Lancashire

Tales of

MYSTERY
& MURDER

Steve Fielding

COUNTRYSIDE BOOKS
NEWBURY BERKSHIRE

First published 2005
© Steve Fielding 2005

COUNTRYSIDE BOOKS
3 Catherine Road
Newbury, Berkshire

To view our complete range of books,
please visit us at
www.countrysidebooks.co.uk

ISBN 1 85306 934 5
EAN 978 1 85306 934 5

Cover design by Peter Davies,
Nautilus Design

Produced through MRM Associates Ltd., Reading
Printed by Arrowsmith, Bristol

Contents

MAP OF LANCASHIRE

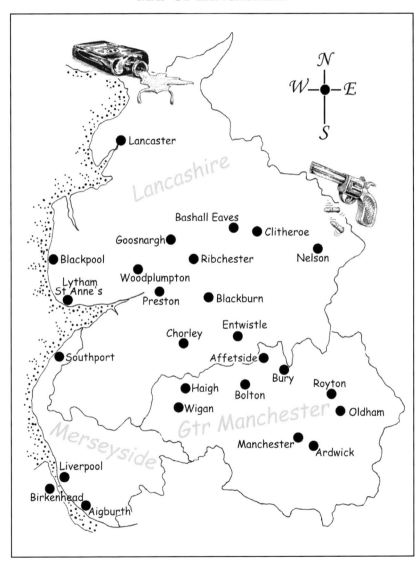

Acknowledgements

I would like to thank the following people for their help in compiling this collection of Lancashire mysteries and murders.

Firstly, Matthew Spicer for help in supplying information and illustrations from his own archives; Rachel Haslam, Katie Haslam and Janet Buckingham for a variety of tasks from proof reading to supplying data, information, illustrations and photographs; and Lisa Moore for help at every stage of the book, in particular with the photographs.

Lastly, my thanks go to Nicholas and Suzanne Battle, and Paula Leigh, for helping me put together this my fifth book for Countryside Books.

THE BODY IN THE FURNACE

The murder of James Barton near Wigan, January 1863

At a little after 6 pm on Friday night, 2nd January 1863, James Barton adjusted his heavy woollen scarf to keep out the cold, left his house and walked to the pit, where he was employed as a tenter on the pumping engine. The colliery belonged to the Earl of Crawford and Bacarres and stood on the Leeds Liverpool canal close to Red Rock Bridge at Haigh, on the Wigan and Chorley border. James worked there, along with several of his sons. As he made the short journey through the darkness he met up with his son, John, who was returning from his shift at the pit; they spoke briefly then went their separate ways. It was the last time James Barton was seen alive.

In the early hours of the following morning, James Watmough, in charge of the pit ponies, went into the pump engine room to collect some burning embers to light a brazier in his own hut. He found the cabin empty with the boiler fire so low that it wasn't generating enough steam to drive the pumping engine. He was not unduly alarmed and, assuming that Barton had gone elsewhere in the colliery to deal with some issue, he stoked up the furnace and got the engine up to steam again. As he was completing this task he noticed something that would set in motion a police investigation that was to last over three years.

Lying on the floor in the corner were the remnants of a burned scarf, similar to one Barton was known to wear. With the light from his lantern he made a further investigation of the cabin and found streaks of blood on the furnace door and, most worryingly, a large crowbar clotted with traces of what also looked like blood.

One of Barton's sons, also called James, was due to take over from his father in the pumping station before dawn. He was summoned to the engine room and a search was carried out of the colliery outbuildings but no trace of Barton was found. They returned to the furnace room where Barton's son opened the firebox door and noticed that the ashes were a very white colour, as if someone had been burning wood instead of coal. Using the furnace rake, he scraped out some ashes and noticed what looked like human bones.

As daylight dawned and word spread that there may have been an horrific murder at the colliery, police officers descended on the scene. Under the command of the Chief Constable of the Lancashire Police, Captain Elgee, officers from Wigan and Chorley made a thorough investigation of the area. Salvaged from the furnace were a number of bones identified by a police surgeon as being part of a human skull, thighbone and a left arm. A chemical analyst from Liverpool was able to state that the residue attached to the clinker was human blood and a quantity of what was found to be body fat was discovered in the grate beneath the furnace. Also recovered were charred remnants of a waistband, brace buckles, some buttons and boot nails.

It seemed clear to the police that a terrible crime had been committed and that the likely victim was the missing engineman, but what was the motive and, more importantly, who had carried out such a dastardly act? The police soon had a lead when it was discovered that a convicted criminal, held in a nearby mental hospital, had escaped from his cell on the night prior to the supposed murder. When it was found that he was a native of Haigh and may well have returned home and therefore have been in the area at the time the crime was committed, finding him became a priority. He was soon rounded up but was then discounted from enquiries.

Detectives believed that robbery was the motive for the crime since missing from the scene was a silver pocket watch, which Barton was known to habitually carry about his person. They also considered that more than one person had carried out the killing and it was this assumption that was to dominate the enquiry for the duration of the investigation. Rumour spread that Barton had been seen in a nearby public house shortly before he disappeared and that he had been witnessed counting a large amount of money.

The pit owner put up a substantial reward for information leading to the arrest of the murderer or murderers and detectives also announced that they would consider a free pardon for any accomplice if they would give a testimony that would lead to the successful conviction of the guilty party.

The only other lead was that this incident could in some way be connected to a spate of petty crimes carried out in the area in the previous year in which a number of thefts had taken place in local mills and businesses. It was the first murder in the area for almost twenty-five years and by coincidence the victim was also an employee at the colliery. Despite the best efforts of the police and the substantial reward on offer, the trail for the killer or killers grew cold and the hunt was scaled down. An inquest was held and a verdict of murder by person or persons unknown was recorded.

It was to be over two years later when an extraordinary chain of events led to the guilty party being arrested. On 12th October 1865, the Governor of Warwick Gaol contacted Superintendent Ellison of the Wigan Police Force with the news that a prisoner in his charge had made a confession that he was involved in the murder at Haigh. Detectives hurried to the Midlands and spoke to John Healey, a Manchester tailor, who told them a remarkable tale.

Healey said that on Friday, 2nd January, 1863, he arrived in Chorley, having walked from Liverpool. Around 6 pm that evening he walked for a couple of hours in the direction of Wigan. During this trek he drank a quantity of ale and took shelter on the road. As he sat in the darkness he was approached by a group of four men with whom he got into conversation. They invited him to join them and, although initially wary, he decided to go for a drink with them in a nearby public house where they shared a bottle of whisky. Healey said that they then passed the Bankhouse Colliery whereupon they entered the grounds and found themselves in the engine house. He then made a chilling declaration:

> 'One of the men got hold of Barton by the neck and gave him a blow with his fist, knocking him down and took his watch and money. We then got him to the fireplace. Barton kicked and struggled very much while the men were putting him in the fire.'

He gave a vague description of the four men, stating that they were all tall and aged in their mid twenties. Healey was removed from the gaol and taken to Wigan, where he was held in a lock-up at Pemberton while his story was checked out.

Following the murder, the police had taken a number of statements, some of which they had not made public. One was from a canal worker who told police she had seen a group of four men on the canal bank in the early hours of Saturday morning, around the time the murder was alleged to have been carried out. So, John Healey's statement, treated with scepticism by some officers, nevertheless, was intriguing enough to warrant closer investigation.

Once ensconced in the Wigan police cell, however, Healey changed his mind about his testimony, but at a subsequent hearing it did not stop the police charging him with the crime and he was remanded to the next assizes.

Hardly had the furore of the arrest died down when, on 13th November, there was a further dramatic development. Sitting in the bar at the Top Lock beerhouse, in Aspull, Thomas Walton, a local labourer, was discussing the confession with the landlord Alexander Shepherd when he made a startling statement:

'Healey knows nothing about it and I can prove it at the trial', he declared. Clearly drunk and of low intelligence, Walton reaffirmed the boast in the presence of a local policeman who Shepherd had asked one of his staff to go and fetch. When asked how he could disprove the confession, Walton claimed that he had been present in the company of several men and that he knew where the dead man's watch had been thrown into the canal.

Taken into custody, he was brought before a hearing at the Moot

Hall in Wigan charged with being connected with the murder. In many ways, his testimony matched that of Healey, except that he denied that the former had any involvement at all in the incident. 'If he was there he was invisible', Walton stated.

Walton declared that he had been drinking with a group of men on Wigan Lane, at a beerhouse called Dychers. At closing time they had bought a quantity of beer and headed towards Bankhouse Pit. He said that as they passed the pit one of the men said he was going to 'see to' Barton whom he blamed for reporting him to the police for poaching on nearby land. 'He was knocked down and I opened the door while the others put him in'. He told police that the man who had carried out the assault had threatened the others with a savage beating if they didn't keep quiet. They had then walked down the

Pendlebury Bridge on the Leeds to Liverpool canal, where Walton alleged the watch was thrown into the water.

canal towards Pendlebury Bridge whereupon they threw the man's watch into the watery depths.

As he was taken to Liverpool to be remanded at Kirkdale Gaol, Walton said that this would be his last journey and that he would be hanged for this, at the same time stating that Healey was innocent and would have to be released.

As a result of these two startling confessions, both independent of each other and both claiming responsibility, it was decided to postpone the forthcoming trial at the winter assizes for further investigations and to reschedule it for the spring. This would also allow time for a search of the canal.

This necessitated a complicated procedure of damming the water between one of the locks and a bridge, and it was to be three months before the operation was fully underway. Under the watchful eyes of detectives on the riverbank, over 100 navvies from the Wigan Waterworks carefully shovelled mud from the riverbed onto platforms where it was then lifted onto the banking to be examined.

While all this was taking place, handbills were made up and distributed describing the missing watch and its unique markings. It was this that was to bring the real felon to justice. Reading the handbill was James Grime, a young man from Chorley, who recognised the watch as one he had had in his possession around the time of the murder.

Grime had been asked to look after the watch by his older brother Thomas, who said he had obtained it in Liverpool a year or so earlier, and he had subsequently pledged it to a pawnbroker in April 1863, using the name John Wallwork. Although police had asked all pawnbrokers in the area to be on the look-out for the stolen watch, it had already been sold to a man called Akers and wasn't recognised as the one belonging to Barton.

Despite knowing that his actions could have grim implications for his brother, who was married with a young son and currently serving three years in Dartmoor for theft, Grime located Akers, reclaimed the watch and in the company of his father they visited Superintendent Ellison at Wigan. From markings inside the case and from the serial number, which he had recorded in his ledger when he last repaired it, a local watchmaker was able to confirm that this was indeed the watch owned by James Barton

Armed with this information, a habeas corpus was issued and detectives travelled to Dartmoor to question Grime where, following a statement he made, he accompanied them back to Lancashire charged with wilful murder.

Once charged, Grime made a further statement, this time implicating two associates, one of whom, Seddon, had subsequently died. In a statement that echoed that of Walton, he said that a man named William Thompson was the killer and that the three men had made their way to the pit because Thompson had a grudge against Barton after he had reported him for poaching, and that after striking him with a metal bar Seddon and Thompson had put him into the furnace. Thompson, although a man of bad conduct with previous convictions for assault, strenuously denied the allegations, but was taken into custody and remanded on suspicion of being implicated in the murder.

By the time the case came before the judge, Mr Baron Martin, at Liverpool in August 1866, charges against everyone except Thomas Grime were dropped and he alone stood in the dock. Grime insisted that his previous statement was correct and that he was guilty only of taking possession of the stolen watch. His counsel referred to the other confessions of murder and said that these supported their client's innocence of carrying out the actual murder.

Grime's fate was effectively sealed, however, when in his summing up the judge pointed out to the jury that, even if they believed his version that he was only present as an accomplice, he was guilty. The jury took just minutes to find that Grime was guilty as charged, believing the prosecution's version of events that it was Grime alone that had carried out the crime.

Pronouncing sentence of death, Baron Martin declared he had no desire to inflict unnecessary pain on the prisoner by dwelling on the details of the crime but it was satisfactorily proved to his mind as if he had seen it committed by the prisoner with his own eyes and, if punishment by death was ever to be inflicted, never had there occurred a case more worthy of it. He therefore held out no hope of a respite and warned the prisoner to do his best to make his peace speedily with God.

Grime was scheduled to be hanged at noon on Saturday, 1st September, in front of Kirkdale Gaol. In the days leading up to the execution he asked to speak to governor Captain Gibbs at the prison and in his presence he made a full confession and stated that he alone had carried out the attack for the purpose of robbery, and that all the others implicated either by his or their own statements were innocent of the crime.

Just twenty-four hours before his execution, however, he asked to see the governor again and this time he said that his last confession was untrue and that it was Thompson who had carried out the attack while he had tried to stop him.

Saturday, 1st September, wasn't a particularly pleasant day. It was cloudy and raining intermittently but, despite this, crowds began to swell outside the gaol from an early hour. Many had caught a special excursion train from Wigan! By the time hangman William Calcraft led the condemned man out onto the scaffold, it was estimated that close on 50,000 people had congregated. As the hangman placed the noose around his neck, Grime declared 'Lord Jesus receive my soul' and he was praying fervently when the drop fell and James Barton was finally avenged.

THE DAY SHE HOPED TO BECOME A WIFE

———— ❃ ————

The murder of Annie Ratcliffe at Preston, August 1881

It ought to have been the happiest day of her young life. Wednesday, 3rd August 1881 had dawned into a warm, sunny morning as 16-year-old Annie Ratcliffe dressed in her finest clothes and set off to meet the man who, in just a few hours, was to become her husband. The rendezvous was the Sir Walter Scott Inn on North Road, Preston and at a little after 8.30 am Annie arrived to find her fiancé Jack Simpson already waiting. But the impending ceremony was not going to be the happy occasion the young bride-to-be had always planned, and her father had given his blessing reluctantly, mainly on account of her heavily pregnant condition.

Jack Simpson had first set eyes on pretty Annie Ratcliffe two years previously when he called into her father's public house, the Blue Bell Inn on Church Street. Infatuated by the pretty young landlord's daughter, Simpson became a regular visitor. The recently widowed Alf Ratcliffe considered his daughter far too young to be courting and, age difference aside, he neither liked nor trusted Simpson. Although clearly well-educated and polite, Simpson was frequently out of work, often living on whatever money he could scrounge or win at the racecourse. After an altercation in a crowded bar one afternoon Ratcliffe accused Simpson of being a lazy fool and a waster and, banned him from the pub, warning his daughter not to see him again.

Forbidden to meet in person, they wrote letters declaring their feelings for each other. Her letters became increasingly fraught at her father's refusal to let them see each other, in one declaring that she would rather die than be unable to see her lover. She pleaded with Simpson to speak to her father and make it clear his feelings for her were genuine, and that if her father would give them his blessing and allow Jack to drink in the Blue Bell, then they would wait until she was eighteen before taking their courtship further.

Simpson took heed of the letter and asked Ratcliffe to change his mind. He told him he had found a job and would stop gambling, but it was to no avail. Rather, the young suitor was told exactly what Alf Ratcliffe thought of him and thrown off the premises, warning him to stay away for good. This attitude by her father only seemed to strengthen their bond. They soon began clandestine assignations, meeting up whenever Simpson could slip away from his job at the registry office, sometimes even three times a day for anything up to an hour at a time. After secretly meeting together for almost two years, the inevitable happened and Annie found herself pregnant.

Initially Annie was filled with horror and fear at her situation, even contemplating suicide at one point. However, she soon realised that her condition would probably mean that her father would now have to accept their relationship and give his blessing to their union. Indeed her father's anger and upset did mellow a little and, as her condition began to show, Alf Ratcliffe finally agreed to sign a consent form acquiescing to their wedding. On 7th July, he reluctantly penned his signature on the document, but told Simpson in no uncertain terms that he would still not be welcome at the pub and that he had no intention of attending the wedding.

Alf Ratcliffe wasn't the only one not looking forward to the nuptials. Annie was so caught up with planning the wedding and trying to win her father's blessing, she failed to notice that Jack Simpson wasn't as enthralled by the impending event as she was, despite saying that he would make arrangements at his office to set a wedding date.

Monday, 1st August 1881 was set as the day and it was at a little after 7.30 am that the couple met outside the Queen's Arms. Annie was wearing her new dress and as Jack ushered her inside she could see something was amiss. He told her he had just received some bad news. The ceremony planned for that morning would have to be postponed until Wednesday, as the registrar wasn't available that day. Seeing his bride's tears, Simpson too began to cry, and both were red eyed when Annie's sister Edith arrived. They left soon after and it was arranged that the three would spend the following day together.

On the Wednesday, Simpson met up with Annie outside the Walter Scott Inn. She was pleased to see that he didn't look as worried as he had on the Monday. As they entered the small saloon in the pub, his smile reassured her that within the next hour or so she would achieve her dream of becoming Mrs Simpson. They sat in the empty bar where the landlady's daughter, 17-year-old Mary Quigley, served them with two lemonades. Mary was struck by the thought that they didn't look like two people who were about to be wed, and a few minutes later she peeped back into the bar to see them both silently staring out of the window.

Ten minutes later the sound of breaking glass caused the young lady to hurry back into the bar, whereupon she saw Annie stagger towards her with blood pouring from her mouth. Mary's screams alerted her mother, who rushed to the bar in time to see Annie stagger and collapse in the doorway. Simpson sat motionless in his chair with a bloodstained razor on the table. 'Who's done this?' the landlady cried. Simpson shook his head quietly before replying, 'I don't know'.

The commotion inside the bar attracted the attention of a passer-by who alerted a nearby policeman. Simpson was immediately placed under arrest. Police surgeon Charles Green arrived at the pub and confirmed that Annie had died from horrific throat wounds. The terrible news spread quickly and, as Annie's body was removed to the mortuary, police officers called at Simpson's house, where his two sisters were just about to depart for the wedding.

As detectives investigated the case several things became apparent. Firstly, that the murder had been premeditated. The razor used to carry out the brutal attack was identified as belonging to a Preston barber whom Simpson had visited on the previous Saturday. The barber had subsequently noticed one of his shaving razors missing and was able to tell police that it bore the inscription 'John Heiffer, Sheffield'. The murder weapon carried this identical marking. Secondly, and most curiously, police found that no plans had in fact been made for the wedding, no one at the registry office had any knowledge of the impending nuptials, neither was the verger at St Paul's church aware that a wedding was to take place.

The trial of John Aspinall Simpson for wilful murder took place before Mr Justice Kay at Manchester Assizes on 7th November. The prosecution's case was straightforward. Simpson had used Annie's infatuation with him to get her to steal money from her father's pub. When she became pregnant and her father gave his permission to allow them to wed, Annie decided she could no longer steal from her father. Simpson, they declared, decided that he would rather murder her than marry her.

Witnesses were called to say that they had overheard a conversation between the young couple in which she had told him she refused to steal for him. One of Simpson's ex-girlfriends told the court that the accused had stated he had no intentions of getting married: 'to hell with marriage, I'm only after the money!'.

The defence version of the events that happened that August morning was two-fold. They made reference to letters Annie had written to her fiancé in which she declared she would rather die if she couldn't be married. They suggested that Simpson had told Annie on the Wednesday morning that the wedding couldn't go ahead and, heartbroken, she had taken her own life. This was dismissed by the prosecution when evidence made it clear that it was Simpson who had carried the razor, one that he had stolen, which suggested premeditation. Secondly, they declared that the accused's actions suggested insanity. 'Wouldn't a sane man have given her the slip and perhaps taken a boat to America?', his counsel declared.

Summing up after the one-day trial, Mr Justice Key dismissed the insanity plea by saying that the defence had called no medical witnesses to support this theory, nor was there any proof that Annie had a razor or had acquired one, adding that a razor is hardly the thing a bride takes to the church on her wedding day! The jury took

The poignant memorial card that was produced by friends of the murdered girl.

a little over twenty minutes to return a guilty verdict. Simpson was duly sentenced to death. The cool, bluff manner he had adopted since his arrest disappeared as the black cap was placed upon the judge's wig, and he was ashen-faced and in shock as he was led from the dock.

Awaiting his fate in the condemned cell, Simpson made no acknowledgement of his guilt. On 27th November, the day before his execution, his sister brought him a note from Annie's father who, although refusing Simpson's request to visit him in gaol, did offer him forgiveness. Unlike the bright sunny morning when Simpson last tasted freedom, it was a dark, dismal, cold morning as he was led to the gallows and hanged expeditiously by William Marwood. His last request was that a photograph of Annie was buried with him.

Why did John Aspinall Simpson murder his young bride-to-be? It seemed clear throughout the period of their courtship that he was very fond of her, whether she was supplying him with money stolen from her father's pub or not. He never explained his actions. A memorial card was produced with a verse printed below the picture of Simpson and Annie Ratcliffe:

That lovely morn I fully hoped I should become a wife
And had no fear that one so dear would take away my life
But death doth come in many forms – though painful was my lot
I pray for those I've left behind, and say, 'forget me not'.

THE 5.15 EXPRESS

---❀---

It was a warm and sunny Saturday afternoon towards the end of July 1940, when the early afternoon passenger train chugged its way up the line in the direction of Blackburn. Looking out of his cabin window near Entwistle station, the signalman noticed a boy aged around six or seven years of age running around in the field of the adjacent farm as if chasing shadows. He was dressed in what he took to be a school uniform – short trousers and a grey pullover.

The railwayman had been in charge of the small signal box on the Bolton to Blackburn railway line for several years and knew most of the residents on the nearby farms. He didn't recognise the youngster, and assumed he was probably a friend or relative who had been evacuated to the area since enemy air raids had made living in the big towns and cities a dangerous thing that summer.

On the following Saturday, at around the same time, he happened to look up as he eased one of the highly polished levers back into position, and again he glimpsed the youngster running across the meadow.

He saw the boy regularly throughout the summer, usually in the late afternoon and always dressed the same. As the nights began to draw in and autumn approached, he saw him less and less. But come the next summer and again he would see him playing in the fields. Many times the young boy was spotted standing close to the crossing gates, his face clearly tinged with sadness, pressed close to the heavy wooden gates as if looking for something or someone.

One warm Saturday in June 1944, the boy had been playing in the field as usual. The signalman had been attending to his duties for

The Bolton to Blackburn railway line.

most of the afternoon and, when he finally glanced across into the field later that day, he saw no one apart from the sheep grazing.

That evening a bell rang in the cabin and accordingly he adjusted the lever and accepted the 4.50 pm from Bolton. The next train through would be the 5.15 pm express heading for Manchester, and it normally entered his sector at 5.01 pm. Today it was several minutes late. With the signal showing amber, the engine slowed as it approached and it wasn't until 5.20 pm that the train finally built up a head of steam and began to ease its way down the line. No sooner had the engine cleared the box window than there was a squeal of brakes, followed by the sound of shouting.

Although still unsure as to the nature of the incident, the signalman put into action his emergency training. He threw the warning signals to red and rang down to the boxes along the line to warn his colleagues to await a further report. Then he stepped out of the cabin and saw that something had happened at the nearby level crossing.

A short time later, a clanging bell heralded the approach of an ambulance to the crossing. The train was able to continue its journey within the hour, but it wasn't until around 8 pm, when his colleague came on duty to take over for the night shift, that he heard what had happened.

'That was a bad business today, wasn't it?' the night watchman muttered, taking off his coat: 'One of the farmers from yon farm by the reservoir it was, went straight under the engine. Fellow called Billy, second one in that family to go that way.'

The signalman stopped at the door.

'You sure? I've been here for over ten years now and it's the first accident I've seen on the line.'

'Oh yes, I'm sure. It was at the end of the last war, around the time of that Zeppelin bomb in Bolton. Bill had an older brother called Harry. Harry was around seven or eight at the time and always playing around in the meadow across the line there.'

He knew what was coming . . .

'Harry used to meet his father's cart as he returned to the farm on Saturday afternoons. He would run down the dirt track and ride the last hundred yards or so alongside his father. One afternoon his father was delayed. Harry played in the fields for a while then waited by the fence. Then he spotted his father approaching, ran down the banking and straight under the 5.15 express.'

There were no further sightings of the young boy on the quiet suburban line.

A Poisoner at
Lancaster Castle

---❖---

The suspicious deaths of Annie Bingham, William Bingham, Margaret Cox and James Bingham at Lancaster Castle, November 1910 – August 1911

William Hodgson Bingham had been the custodian of Lancaster Castle for over thirty years. He was a wealthy man, well-respected by all who knew him and popular with the staff and visitors at the castle. That is until he was beset by a series of tragedies that passed the family name into the annals of crime.

In November 1910, at the age of seventy-three, William Bingham still worked daily at the castle as both keeper and guide. A widower for many years, he lived with his children, several of whom worked in the castle.

The mysterious deaths began one chilly winter morning on 12th December 1910 when his 30-year-old daughter Gertrude 'Annie' Bingham died suddenly. The doctor who examined the body stated that cause of death was 'cerebral congestion and hysteria'.

No sooner had this tragedy struck than the family suffered a further loss; this time it was William himself who, on 22nd January 1912, succumbed to 'gastro-enteritis' after a thirty-six hour bout of vomiting and diarrhoea. As the old man had been active and in good health, his death came as a terrible shock, following as it did so soon after that of his daughter.

William's son James took over his father's role as custodian of the castle and things went back to normal until July, when James's

William Bingham.

widowed stepsister Margaret Cox resigned her job at a local asylum and came to live and work at the castle, replacing the recently departed housekeeper. She had been at the castle for less than a week when she, too, was suddenly struck down. Although her symptoms were similar in many ways to that of her father, cause of death in her case was recorded as 'cerebral haemorrhaging'.

Needing a replacement housekeeper as a matter of urgency, James asked his sister Edith Agnes Bingham to take on the position. She wasn't his ideal choice as the two of them weren't on the best of terms, and this situation proved difficult when they began to quarrel daily: he criticising her attitude to the role and the time she spent away from work with her suitor. After less than one month in the job, Edith was relieved of her duties and a replacement housekeeper was sought.

James, along with some servants, worked on at the castle while Edith worked her notice period. Then, on 11th August, a few days before a new housekeeper was due to start, James suddenly collapsed with stomach pains just as he was escorting a party around the castle. Dr McIntosh was summoned and at once his suspicions were aroused. Already aware that three members of the family had died suddenly over the last six months, the collapse of the erstwhile healthy James Bingham convinced him that something sinister was afoot. Bingham had eaten a meal of beefsteak, bread and tea prepared by his sister Edith and within the hour had been taken ill.

Samples of the sick man's vomit were sent to Liverpool for analysis and word soon came back that they contained a large dose of arsenic. James seemed to rally after his initial collapse but four days later, on

15th August, he became the fourth member of his family to die suddenly in the last eight months.

The police were alerted and Inspector Whitfield and Detective Sergeant Johnson of the Lancaster Constabulary took over the investigation. They soon found two empty tins of Acme weed killer containing arsenic in a rubbish hole near to the Judge's entrance to the castle, covered by rusty chains. The tins were labelled as poison. It was, however, no secret to the staff at the castle that both James and his father had used the poison liberally around the castle grounds to control weeds.

A post-mortem examination could not find a natural cause of death and, in ordering an inquest to be carried out, the coroner also made arrangements for the bodies of William and Margaret Bingham to be exhumed. Samples of tissue from the stomach were sent to

Lancaster castle where all the victims worked.

Liverpool for analysis by Dr Collingwood-Williams and his assistant Mr W. H. Roberts. They, too, were found to contain white arsenic – the same poison as discovered in the weed killer tins.

At the subsequent inquest, further evidence of poisoning came from James Bingham's doctor who said that whilst he was attending his patient he had immediately suspected poisoning. William Bingham junior also testified and when asked about his sister Edith he stated that in his opinion she was of weak intellect. Their sister Nellie Bingham also gave evidence that her sister was unhappy with her treatment at the castle and asked to be allowed to live with Nellie in Manchester. The inquest ended with the jury finding that James Bingham had died as a result of arsenic poisoning administered by his sister. Edith Bingham was remanded in custody.

Her subsequent trial for wilful murder was held at Lancaster Assizes before Mr Justice Avory on 27th October 1911, in the very courtroom where Edith had worked as an attendant in the ladies gallery for several years. She was charged with three counts of murder, that of her father William Hodgson Bingham in January, her half-sister Margaret in July and finally her brother James in August, 1911.

Mr Langdon KC and Mr Gordon Hewart led for the prosecution, whilst Mr Wingate-Saul and Mr Sellers acted for the defence. The prosecution's case was based mainly on circumstantial evidence, providing means, motive and opportunity. William junior was again called as a witness. He acknowledged that Edith and James had frequently argued before his death but agreed that this was because she paid scant attention to her duties, and that when she did carry them out, 'her inclination was to go about them in an expensive way'.

The prosecution called forward Charles Emerson, Edith's fiancé. The prosecution alleged that she had lured him into an engagement on the promise that she had property in Morecambe, and to support this claim she had therefore to attempt to obtain property quickly in order to keep her man. Emerson, when called to the stand, said that although it was commonly believed amongst friends that they were engaged, it had never been made official and there was no understanding between them. He said he was aware that she had told him lies about property and her inheritance.

Scientific evidence suggested that in all cases death was due to poisoning by arsenic. Analysis of the weed killer found near the castle showed that it contained ninety-seven grains of white arsenic per fluid ounce. Various samples taken from around the family house, from the wallpaper to water samples, all came back clear of arsenic. It seemed that the prosecution had provided means and motive: access to poison for the means, and a need to obtain property as motive.

Members of the domestic staff were called to support the prosecution case and one of the charwomen took the stand to provide opportunity. She stated that she had seen the accused preparing a beefsteak stew for James on 12th August, and that she later saw James after he was taken ill, only an hour after eating the stew. When asked if she had seen Edith eating the stew, she replied that she had not. When asked if she had seen Edith eating meat on occasions previous to 12th August, she answered that she had. She could not, therefore, explain why Edith had not, on that occasion, eaten the stew.

Despite all the evidence that seemed to be against Edith, the defence did not call a single witness. Wingate Saul stated that it was not for him to prove how James died, but for the prosecution to prove, beyond reasonable doubt, that Edith wilfully put arsenic into the stew she fed to James. He then stated that the motive provided by the prosecution, that Edith killed her family for money, was not credible. Following the death of her brother, Edith would not gain financially as any inheritance from his death would pass to William junior, and that she would, in fact, be in a worse state both emotionally and financially by the loss of her brother.

In summing up, Mr Justice Avory stated that the prosecution did not need to supply a motive, as death by poisoning in itself implied malice. However, the prosecution did need to prove that Edith knowingly introduced the arsenic into the food, and, if so, was it her intent to kill him or just to harm him? He suggested that the prosecution had provided no real evidence as to how Edith administered the poison to the food of her father and half sister, if indeed she did. After a deliberation that took only twenty minutes, the jury returned. They found the defendant not guilty on all three counts.

The case of the Lancaster Poisoning remains an unsolved mystery. Reading through the facts as they appeared in the newspapers of the day, it is clear that the amount of circumstantial evidence would be enough in many cases to secure a conviction. Did a guilty murderess evade justice? We will never know.

EQUALLY GUILTY

———————— ❖ ————————

The Murder of Daniel Bardsley at Oldham, December 1913

I am sorry to be obliged to refuse to see you. I have given the fullest and most anxious consideration to the representations which have been made to me to mitigate the sentence passed on Kelly, and I deeply regret that I can come to no other decision than that which has been conveyed to you, and it must be regarded as final.

R McKenna
Home Secretary

It was Tuesday evening, 16th December 1913, and the streets of Oldham had an air of menace. There was anger and frustration at the news that had just reached them from the Home Secretary's office and, as they congregated outside the family home of a young man who had less than twelve hours to live, the anger reached fever pitch. Many stood in tears while the mother of the condemned man seemed in a state of total collapse, moaning incoherently that her son was being treated unfairly.

As realisation set in that the law was going to take its course, the mob marched towards the town hall smashing windows and chanting angrily, venting their wrath at the Home Secretary. As more people joined the throng, many the worse for drink, police were on full alert and as the crowd surrounded Werneth Police Station, the situation became critical. Bricks were hurled through windows as officers were summoned from surrounding districts, and it took ranks of mounted police to drive the crowds back. As the pubs emptied the crowd swelled, many shouting and gesturing, vowing 'no work tomorrow', as they continued to throw missiles and verbally abuse the police. Not content with smashing shop windows they began to attack trams and several police were violently assaulted as they tried to break up the mêleé.

It was as midnight approached that someone made the decision to march on Strangeways prison. With the mob growing by the minute, word was sent ahead and police reinforcements from all across Lancashire hurried to give assistance. Arriving at the prison and having armed themselves with sticks, crowbars and a variety of shovels and spades, the angry mob reached the end of Southall Street opposite the prison gates. A standoff commenced as dawn broke out over the grim Victorian gaol.

As 8 o'clock approached, inside the prison the condemned man prayed fervently in his cell. As the hour struck, hangman John Ellis and his assistant entered the condemned cell and after thanking the governor and staff for their kindness, the prisoner strode bravely onto the trapdoor and seconds later paid the full penalty for a brutal crime. So what had caused such a furore?

Daniel Wright Bardsley had run a profitable bookselling and stationery business on Oldham's bustling Yorkshire Street. Having thrown himself fully into the business, he found himself at 54 years of age a confirmed bachelor, sharing his home with his brother. He employed a staff of three: two women, Annie Leech and Clara Hall, and 17-year-old Edward Wild Hilton who worked as a packer and errand boy. Hilton had only been employed at the shop for a few weeks since returning to his native Oldham from Canada, having spent time in a special school there for children with learning difficulties. His work was not satisfactory and on Saturday, 26th July, at the close of business, Bardsley called him into the office and told him finally he would have to let him go. Hilton had been given this news earlier in the day but had pleaded for a second chance, promising to 'shape up'. Bardsley had said he would think about it, but having watched him go about his duties that afternoon he felt that he was not suited to the business.

In the early hours of the following morning, James Greaves, a

Daniel Bardsley's shop in Oldham (© Oldham Local Studies and Archive).

night watchman whose duties took in the premises along Yorkshire Street, noticed the back door of Bardsley's shop ajar and shining his torch inside saw the body of a man lying on the packing room floor. He hurried to the local police station and officers accompanied him back to the premises. Inspector Johnson gained entry into the store and found Daniel Bardsley lying face down in a pool of blood. It was clear he had suffered a fearful beating: his face was swollen and discoloured and there were streaks of blood on the floor and walls. Beside the body were a metal dumb-bell and a wooden Indian club, both of which were covered in blood.

Shortly after dawn that Sunday morning, Johnson spoke to both the female employees at the bookstore. They each confirmed that they had left Bardsley working in the upstairs office at around 10.30 pm the previous evening. Hilton had helped secure the shutters on the front of the shop and had left shortly before them, at around 10.10 pm. Clara Hall also mentioned a few things that suggested a potential motive: she told officers that earlier that previous afternoon she had gone to a local jeweller to collect half a dozen sovereign rings, so that Bardsley could chose one for himself without having to leave the premises. She also mentioned that she was present when her boss had told the young lad Hilton that he was terminating his employment, and that the rings had been on the desk when that conversation took place.

Hilton was interviewed at his home later that morning. He seemed shocked and upset when told the tragic news and was asked for his movements after he finished work. Avoiding eye contact, Hilton said he had met his friend Ernie outside the shop and that they had gone to the fair at Hollinwood. He said he had returned home shortly after midnight and gone straight to bed. Johnson asked where he could find Ernie but Hilton replied that he didn't know his proper name nor where he lived.

As Johnson spoke to Hilton, a constable went upstairs and noticed on the bedroom floor items of clothing clearly covered in blood. Satisfied that Hilton had been involved in the crime, he was then placed under arrest and taken to the police station, situated at the local town hall.

The friend 'Ernie' with whom Hilton claimed to have spent the evening was soon found to be Ernest Edward Kelly. He was a 20-year-old piecer who worked at Platt Brothers, a local cotton mill, and lived on nearby Ward Street. Inspector Piggott and Detective Jones went to speak to Kelly who, after making an initial denial, admitted that he had struck Bardsley twice with the wooden club but that he was still alive when he left the shop. He took officers into the backyard at the house and showed them where he had stashed a quantity of money and four sovereign rings he had taken from the office.

Kelly was taken to the police station and, with the two young men face to face, they each blamed the other for carrying out the fatal blows. Hilton took the officers back to his house and showed them where he had hidden his share of the spoils.

On the following day an inquest was held which found that Daniel Bardsley had died after being struck several times about the head by a blunt instrument and that either or both weapons found beside the body could have made the wounds. The short hearing ended with both men being remanded to stand trial at the winter assizes.

Mr Justice Avory presided over the trial at Manchester Assizes which opened on Monday, 24th November. Mr Gordon Hewart, KC MP, led for the Crown and outlined the prosecution's case that both men were concerned in the robbery of the bookstore and that during the furtherance of the theft they had committed a brutal murder.

Represented by Mr M'Cleary, Hilton was the first to take the stand. He admitted that he was influenced by watching cowboy films, that he sometimes carried a replica cowboy pistol, both he and Kelly were fond of watching westerns at the cinema, and that on the night of the murder he had been dismissed from his position at the shop. He said that he had arranged to meet Kelly after work and that they had intended to go to Hollinwood Fair. However, they had a problem as neither of them had any money, and when Hilton said he had been sacked from his job, it was Kelly who suggested that they commit the robbery. Hilton said he had wanted to wait until his former boss had locked up but Kelly suggested they went straight round to save having to break in.

While they debated what to do, Kelly had disappeared for ten minutes and Hilton's defence claimed he used this time to go and collect the wooden Indian club he kept in his yard. Hilton went on to describe how they waited until the two female assistants who worked at the shop had left and he then went in. When Bardsley asked him what he wanted, he said he had come to pick up his apron. Clearly annoyed, he was told to collect it and go. Hilton said that as he went into the back room to get it he suddenly heard a cry and spinning round he saw that Kelly was standing over the unconscious man holding the bloodstained club.

Aghast, Hilton shrieked 'Oh no, God will punish us for this,' and said that it was the first time he had seen the club. Kelly asked where the safe was and on being told it was in the office upstairs they both hurried up and attempted to force it open. It was at this point that they heard the moaning and stumbling from downstairs as Bardsley recovered from the blow and was attempting to get to his feet.

Hilton said he went downstairs and tried to revive the victim with a drink of water. He shouted for Kelly to help him and as the older youth came downstairs he walked over to the stricken bookseller where, instead of offering assistance, he picked up the wooden club and brought it down with great force onto his head. As the man struggled, Kelly was alleged to have forced a handkerchief into his mouth to stifle the moans. Leaving him for dead they rifled his pockets, taking the money from his wallet and a bunch of keys that they used in a vain attempt to open the safe. They had then decided to take just the tray of rings off the desk and the contents of the wallet and flee.

Under cross-examination Hilton denied at any time striking any of the blows, blaming that entirely on his accomplice in the dock.

Kelly's version of events was totally different. He agreed that they had arranged to meet after Hilton finished work, but it was Hilton who suggested they carry out the robbery in revenge for having been dismissed. Kelly said that Hilton had suggested he fetch the wooden club in case they needed a weapon to scare him into handing over the

*Kelly and Hilton were fascinated with old cowboy films. They posed
for this picture a few days before committing a brutal murder.*

money. He said that as they waited for the women to leave work,
Hilton had passed him a handkerchief which he suggested he use to
cover his face, while he did the same.

Kelly then recounted how Hilton had told him to take off his
shoes and they crept quietly into the shop. 'Swap jackets with me,'
he had breathed, telling Kelly to make sure he hit him hard with the
club. Asked why they couldn't carry out the robbery without

resorting to violence, Hilton had told him that they would need to get the keys from his pocket and they would need to knock him out to do that.

Kelly said that they were disturbed by Bardsley as they rummaged around the packing room, whereupon Hilton pulled out his replica gun and told him to 'stick-em-up'. Bardsley panicked and tried to flee, making for the back door when he tripped and fell to the ground. At this point, Kelly admitted he had struck the bookseller to try to quieten him down. As he was trying to make him comfortable, Hilton took the club from him and struck him several times about the head before emptying his pockets. He also picked up a tray of rings that had fallen from Bardsley's pocket and then having made a failed attempt to open the safe they slipped out of the back door, divided up the spoils and went their separate ways home.

Summing up the case, Mr Justice Avory told the jury that it didn't matter who struck the fatal blow if both youths had been present when the blows were struck. If both had been present on a joint venture then both were equally guilty. The jury needed just fifteen minutes to return a guilty verdict, adding a recommendation for mercy on account of their youth. With a black cap draped across his wig, Mr Justice Avory sentenced both men to death by hanging.

Hilton had recently turned eighteen and was therefore liable to the death penalty but it was soon announced that as he was under the age of eighteen at the time of the murder his sentence be commuted to life imprisonment. This caused a great deal of outrage amongst the folk of Oldham. Despite the brutal savagery of the attack, many believed it was Hilton who was the more guilty and that if anyone should have been reprieved it should have been Kelly. Numerous petitions were gathered, some collecting many thousand of signatures.

Protestations went on as the date for the execution drew nearer. Members of Parliament were lobbied and letters were sent to Queen Mary, including one from Kelly's mother who described her son as 'the less guilty of the two'. Kelly's representatives also produced evidence that the condemned man was immature, with the mental age of a fourteen-year-old. They showed a photograph taken just a few days before the murder in which Hilton and Kelly posed child-like, dressed as cowboys. It was all to no avail.

And so Ernie Kelly went bravely to the gallows. There was no doubt that he was guilty as charged, as the law stood. It was shown many years later in the Derek Bentley case, that where two men go out to commit a crime, even if they carry no active part in any assault they are deemed equally guilty. The question here wasn't so much was justice done, but rather why was the punishment so unequal.

In Oldham, shortly after the execution a mourning card was produced that stated: 'In loving memory of Ernest Kelly, who was executed at Strangeways Prison, Manchester on December 17th, 1913, notwithstanding the protests of over fifty thousand citizens of Oldham.'

Edward Wild Hilton was released on 9th September 1933, serving almost twenty years for his part in the murder that almost caused a riot.

THE EXECUTIONER'S REVENGE

———————— ❖ ————————

High on the moors overlooking east Lancashire stands the village of Affetside, a small hamlet clustered around the Roman road of Watling Street, which links Manchester to Ribchester. At the centre of the village is the Pack Horse pub, built in 1443, and home to a curious object that is a talking point to all who see it, perched on the shelf above the line of optics behind the bar. It is a skull and, while it is a popular attraction today, its roots lie in tragic events that took place at the height of the civil war when the whole country, and in particular Lancashire, was in turmoil.

Bolton 1651, and civil war raged. On one side were the Roundheads, followers of Cromwell and his Parliamentary forces, and on the other the Royalist supporters of King Charles I.

James Stanley, the 7th Earl of Derby, was a staunch Royalist. He was born in 1607, into a powerful and influential family at Knowsley, and he grew up enjoying a life of privilege and status. At the age of 18 he was elected Member of Parliament for Liverpool and, by the time civil war broke out in 1642, he had became the Lord Lieutenant of Lancashire and Cheshire and had inherited the earldom of Derby.

Lancashire was a torn county: neighbouring towns declared loyalty to opposing sides. Bolton, in line with other partly industrialised communities such as Manchester, was filled with staunch Parliamentary supporters, while rural areas like Preston and Wigan were loyal to the king.

Stanley based his military command at Wigan but, despite his rank and status, his only victory of any merit during the early years of the

The Pack Horse Inn, home to the Affetside skull.

war was at Westhoughton, where a large number of Parliamentarians were taken prisoner. In 1643, he launched two assaults against Bolton, each with little effect. However, his third and most brutal assault, resulted in mass bloodshed. It was this assault that was later condemned as a criminal act, and ultimately cost the earl his life.

The first attack on Bolton came on 16th February 1643, when sixteen people were killed in skirmishes. It was short and swift with the Royalists beaten back in less than four hours. A second Royalist attack took place a year later, in March 1644. It was led by the earl and Captain Anderton of Lostock Hall, and took place at nightfall. This time there were 23 Royalists dead and, as before, there were no Parliamentarian casualties.

A few months later, the earl called for help from his cousin, the king's nephew Prince Rupert, in a final attempt to take Bolton. This time his forces numbered over 12,000. Defended by barely 2,000 Roundheads, the first assault was valiantly beaten off. The second raid, however, was a ruthlessly successful Royalist victory, with almost 2,000 people massacred and much of the town destroyed.

Although the Royalists had conquered Bolton and many other parts of the north-west, they did not win the war. In 1649, King Charles I was beheaded and the throne abolished. Parliament condemned the taking of Bolton as a crime and Cromwell himself demanded the death penalty for the Earl of Derby, who had fled to the Isle of Man.

With a strong army of Manx militia the earl returned to England in 1651 to help the Prince of Wales regain the throne. He was captured at Worcester and court-martialled on grounds of high treason. He was executed on 15th October 1651. His body is buried in Ormskirk where he later became known as the 'martyr Earl of Derby'.

The man who wielded the headsman's axe that autumn morning was George Wherwell, who worked and lived in the Affetside area. He was a hardworking family man who, like the majority of local working folk, supported the Parliamentarians.

Wherwell and his family had been attacked by Royalist troops in the fierce raid on Bolton in the spring of 1644 and, during the attack, he had been forced to watch the raiders ravage his daughter and slaughter a relative. Following the Earl of Derby's court-martial, Wherwell volunteered to be the executioner and, on a scaffold erected on Churchgate, in Bolton town centre, he beheaded the earl with one swift stroke. Yet this beheading was to cost him his life. Several years later, with the monarchy restored, executioner Wherwell's fate was sealed. In an act of revenge, Royalists cut the man's head off and displayed it on a pike outside the Pack Horse as a warning to travellers along the road. It was later taken down and, although nobody is certain when, appeared behind the bar.

A monument and plaque stand in Churchgate marking the spot outside the Man and Scythe public house where Lord Derby spent his last night; a few miles away a fragile, tobacco-stained, skull sits on a shelf high up above a bar. They remain as two gruesome reminders of one of the bloodiest episodes in the county's history.

THE ACT OF A MADMAN?

──────── ❂ ────────

The murder of Kathleen Breaks at Lytham St Anne's, Christmas 1919

It was a farmer who made the gruesome discovery. On the morning of Christmas Eve 1919, after the strong winds and heavy rains of the previous night had died down, Tom Gillett was out on a morning stroll when he noticed two sets of footprints in the wet sand leading towards the sand hills at St Anne's. He followed them to the top of a small dune where he stumbled across the body. She had been shot dead. Lying next to the body was a bloodstained man's glove and a woman's handbag.

Gillett quickly summoned the police and the body was identified from papers in the nearby handbag as being that of Kathleen 'Kitty' Harriet Breaks, aged 28. There was still money in the handbag, which seemingly ruled out robbery as a motive, however, there was also a collection of love letters all signed 'Eric'.

A search of the beach soon uncovered a revolver, shallowly buried in a nearby sand hill. The serial number had been erased from the cylinder but a series of numbers stamped on the hand strap had been overlooked. The weapon was soon traced to a Preston gunsmith, who told detectives that he had sold it to a soldier Frederick 'Eric' Rothwell Holt in 1914. A check into his background found that Holt had been called up as an officer in the Territorial Army at the start of the Great War in August 1914. After taking part in some of the war's bloodiest battles in France, he was invalided out suffering from 'shell shock' and rheumatism. Holt worked briefly in Malaya before returning to his native Blackpool in 1918.

Frederick 'Eric' Holt had served in France during the Great War.

In the early hours of Christmas Day 1919, detectives led by Superintendent Foster called at the house in Blackpool where Holt was staying with his parents. A search of his room found a pair of shoes still caked in sand. These were taken away and were found to be an identical match to the cast made from the clear set of footprints discovered in the wet sand at the scene of the murder. He was taken into custody and charged with murder. While remanded in custody, detectives looked to find a reason for what at first seemed a motiveless crime.

Kitty Breaks met Eric Holt at Middlesborough when she was living apart from her husband John Stoddart Briggs, a garage proprietor from Bridlington. Born in Bristol, she was a very attractive, clever and charming lady and had married Briggs at Bradford in November 1913. They had a tempestuous relationship, mainly on account of the fact that Kitty was something of a nymphomaniac, and the marriage ended after just a few months when he quickly grew tired of her many affairs.

Eric and Kitty soon fell in love and with her living in Bradford he made frequent trips from his home in Blackpool to spend weekends with her. The courtship was passionate and she wrote him scores of letters declaring her love for Holt whom she called her 'Superman'.

On 30th May 1919, Eric Holt had approached the Atlas Insurance Company to enquire about taking out an insurance policy on Kitty for £10,000. His request was refused, mainly because as he was not married to her he could have no claim on her estate if she were to die.

Two months before her death, on 14th October, Holt managed to insure Kitty for £5,000 with a different company, but unsuccessfully tried to take out a further two policies for £10,000 each. Holt had also persuaded Kitty to make her will in his favour, which she signed on 17th December, a week before her death.

On 22nd December, Holt travelled to Bradford and spent the night with Kitty Breaks at her lodgings. On the following day she took possession of the insurance policy and they travelled back together to Blackpool. She arranged to meet Holt later that night at St Anne's. Her body was discovered the following morning.

Holt and Kitty Breaks made a handsome couple.

Frederick Holt stood before Mr Justice Greer in February 1920 at Manchester Assizes. Although his fate looked grim, he had arguably one of the best defence counsels of his time, Sir Edward Marshall Hall, in his corner. But the Crown had a strong leader too, in the form of Attorney General Sir Gordon Hewart.

Marshall Hall's first line of defence was to contend that Holt was mentally unfit to plead. He made this declaration before proceedings began, hoping that if successful it would render the murder trial unnecessary. The defence revealed that both Holt's cousin and grandfather had been committed to a mental asylum. Holt's behaviour since his arrest had also been strange: he had complained that the police were sending huge flying insects carrying deadly germs and dogs to attack him.

However, the jury at the preliminary hearing chose to believe that

Sir Edward Marshall Hall, one of the best defence counsels of his time.

all this 'madness' was a pretence to support a defence of not guilty by reason of insanity.

A fresh jury was then sworn in and the trial began in earnest. It soon became clear that Marshall Hall faced a very difficult task; the damning evidence against Holt was substantial. Marshall Hall had a 'Plan B' when the insanity plea failed, and set about establishing an alibi for Frederick Holt. It was futile: there was nothing or no one to vouch for him on the night of the murder. Holt, as if to reinforce his plea of insanity, sat in the dock with arms folded looking totally disinterested in the whole proceedings. Apart from complaining about the deadly flies he made no attempt to co-operate with either his counsel or solicitor.

The only time he showed any emotion during proceedings was on the fifth day when, during Marshall Hall's impassioned speech about the murdered woman, Holt's eyes brimmed with tears.

In what was to be one of the most impressive and moving speeches of his long career at the bar, Marshall Hall rounded on the crowded public gallery, filled with many fashionable young ladies:

> 'It makes one's heart ache to see that gallery packed with women. It makes me feel sick for the femininity of this country that women should come here, in their furs and their diamonds, day after day, to gloat over the troubles of some poor demented wretch on trial for his life.'

Marshall Hall read Holt's last letter to Kitty, written on the day before she was murdered:

> 'My darling Kathleen, you have no idea how lonely I feel without you, dearest . . . you are the one and only to me in this world . . . I long for some good Christmases with you in times to come and I feel that some time there will be no parting us.'

Hall spoke without notes for more than two hours before finally he sat down. The court was in hushed silence and the judge and half the jury were in tears. But any sympathy he might have elicited from the jury was ruthlessly smashed in a fierce closing speech by the Attorney General and the unsympathetic summing up by Mr Justice Greer. After a five-day trial it took less than an hour for the jury to find him guilty as charged.

When Holt was led back into court to hear the sentence of death passed on him, he was clearly seen stuffing a newspaper into his pocket. Asked if he had anything to say before sentence of death was passed, he shrugged his shoulders, shook his head and looked at the clock. After sentence was passed, he glanced quickly around the court and left the dock: 'Well I'm glad that's over, I hope my tea won't be late' he said to the guards as he returned to the cell.

Marshall Hall was convinced his client was insane and made strenuous efforts to get the verdict overturned. It was in vain. Prior to Holt's execution on 13th April 1920, Marshall Hall wrote to Holt's solicitors:

> 'I feel so strongly that he is now mad, and, as a man, contemplate with horror the idea of executing a madman, that I am willing you should, if you think fit, to communicate the contents of this letter to the Home Secretary or to the Attorney General. As you know I have never had any doubts in my own mind that Holt's hand fired the shot that killed Mrs Breaks, nor have I ever had any real doubt that the deed was done under the influence of some uncontrollable passion acting on a mind enfeebled by shell shock and disease.'

Holt remained indifferent to the campaigns for a reprieve that his family were orchestrating outside the prison walls. On the afternoon before the execution, hangman John Ellis and his assistant William Willis arrived at the prison to prepare for their duties on the following morning. As Ellis watched Holt at exercise he noted that he was a fine, strapping six-footer who looked like an athlete in training as he strode around the exercise yard with the warders huffing and puffing in his wake.

During discussion with one of the prison officers, Ellis asked if they believed Holt really was insane. 'He's not mad at all,' he was told, 'all he has done since he came into the condemned cell is complain. We'll all be glad when it's over and he is gone!'

At 8 am on the following morning the hangmen entered the cell. Holt was standing facing the door with a cigarette dangling between his lips as they approached to pinion his arms. Holt glared at them as they took his arm: 'Is this really necessary?' Ellis replied it was, as he fixed his straps. Holt repeated the question to the Chief Warder standing across the table and, when told it was, he clenched his fists as if to try to pull free. He walked slowly towards the scaffold then stopped a few feet short of the drop. He glared at Ellis and refused to move. Willis gave him a gentle push and they managed to get him under the beam. As Ellis went to place the cotton bag over his head Holt again complained: 'You're not going to put that on!' 'Oh yes I must,' Ellis replied standing on his tiptoes to reach. Ellis said that the last look from Holt was one of sheer hatred. Seconds later with the noose secured, he darted to the lever and the trapdoor crashed open.

'Well that's the last we'll see of him,' muttered one of the warders, 'and I'm not sorry to see him go'.

Was Eric Holt insane as his counsel claimed? He had made no attempt to cover his tracks following the brutal slaying on the sand hills, and if he had committed the murder for the money on the insurance policy he must surely have known that he hadn't a hope of escaping detection. Surely the act of a madman.

THE GYPSY PROPHECY

The murder of Reuben Mort at Bolton, January 1920

At 4.20 am, Jack Lomax and his wife were woken by the sound of banging coming from next door. They dressed quickly and went to summon their neighbour's former housekeeper, Mrs Davies who lived around the corner and had keys to Reuben Mort's hardware and blacksmith's shop at 3 Market Street.

To the folk of Little Lever, a small colliery village on the outskirts of Bolton, he was 'Old Reuben', a kindly bachelor and ex-councillor. At 78-years-old, Reuben Mort still made for an imposing figure, standing well over six foot tall and having a stocky build. Although teased by the local children on occasion and thought a bit peculiar by some of his neighbours, he was generally considered to be without an enemy in the world.

The previous evening, Sunday, 18th January 1920, Mort had been visited by his nephew, James Stringfellow, who ran his own drapery business on the nearby High Street. They chatted for a while and, after sharing a drink, James bid his uncle goodnight and returned home.

When Mr and Mrs Lomax, who ran the local tripe shop, returned to the shop with Mrs Davies in the early hours of Monday morning, they saw that the wooden board the old man had fixed over a window, damaged by a storm just before Christmas, had been pulled away. Mr Lomax shouted inside and heard the old man mumble something before sliding open the lock on the door. They recoiled back in horror at the sight that greeted them. The old man's face was streaming with blood, and there was a trail of blood across the oilcloth floor leading into the sitting room at the back.

Mort was a man of habit and at 3 am he had woken as usual and set about making himself a cup of tea whilst stoking up the fire in the forge, ready for business in the morning. While he was doing this, he looked round and saw a tall stranger wearing a mask. The man demanded the keys to the safe that stood in the corner.

'I don't have them,' Mort told him. 'I don't believe you,' the masked man snarled, and when Mort reaffirmed that they weren't on the premises the intruder pulled out a cosh and approached: 'In that case I will kill you,' he declared raining a series of fierce blows on the old man.

Whilst Mrs Davies hurried to fetch Dr Nuttall who lived close by, Lomax comforted the old man while his wife summoned the police. Before arranging for Mort to be taken to Bolton Infirmary, officers questioned him about the attacker. Apart from saying he was tall and wore a mask, he said he couldn't recognise him and didn't think he would be able to if he saw him again.

Soon after being admitted to hospital, Rueben Mort died from his injuries and a murder investigation began. It was clear that the attacker had made a search of the house, presumably trying to locate the keys. He had neglected to search a cupboard in the kitchen and there hanging on a nail were the keys he had been searching for. Inside the safe was a vast amount of money; over £2,000 in notes.

Robbery was clearly the motive and, as locals were questioned, it became clear that the rumours of the old man's wealth were indeed true. Police discovered he owned several properties in the village as well as having a considerable amount of money. The investigation soon ground to a halt. Although the police received several tip-offs and swooped on a number of properties there was nothing to link anyone to the murder. The best clue they could come up with was that a traveller from a fairground had been seen loitering in Little Lever town centre on the afternoon of the murder. Various people gave vague descriptions of him, and several agreed that he was a tall man, but other than that there was nothing. Local police called in Scotland Yard for advice, and relatives of the murdered man put up a substantial reward of £100 for information leading to the arrest of the killer. A local 'retired' burglar contacted the police and offered his assistance, claiming he had experience that may be useful to their investigation. However, after ruling him out of their enquiries, they politely refused the offer.

On 23rd January the funeral took place of Reuben Mort at St Matthew's church. The cortege left from the home of Mort's nephew, James Stringfellow, and there was what the local newspaper reported at the time as an 'exciting incident'. As the procession formed to make its way to the church, the horses pulling the first coach refused to budge. No amount of coaxing and persuading could get them to move and finally the mourners had to climb out of the carriage and walk behind the hearse on foot.

Word spread that it was due to a local superstition that the horses failed to move because the eyes of the murderer were on the procession. It was rumoured that an old gypsy woman living near the village had prophesised that this would happen!

A week after the funeral took place, an inquest was held in Bolton. The coroner, Mr J. Fearnley, returned a verdict of 'murder by person or persons unknown'. He told the packed assembly that he could only deal with actual evidence brought before him and he did not propose to listen to the numerous rumours that had been sweeping the district. Pretty much every male over the age of sixteen who had been standing watching the funeral possession, had at some point been mentioned as the potential murderer.

'You will probably have heard all sorts of silly idiotic rumours – such a person has done it – even such cruel rumours that relatives have done it,' he said, stating that he was making this announcement as he believed it cruel of people to make suggestions of that description.

Investigations went on for the rest of the year and enquiries took officers to all parts of the county. Finally the hunt was scaled down and reluctantly the dossier was filed as unsolved. The dust on the file was periodically brushed off when some fresh lead emerged but, like others before it, it soon amounted to nothing.

Thus, the killer of Reuben Mort was never brought to justice and the case remains open, as an unsolved murder case is never closed. Who was the killer? Who was the mysterious gypsy type seen in the area shortly before the murder? And was the killer one of those paying their respects as the cortege assembled before the funeral. Like the detectives investigating in 1920, we will never know.

THE VILLAGE THAT HID
A MURDERER

The Murder of James Dawson at Bashall Eaves, March 1934

The world-renowned firearms expert, Robert Churchill, called it his most baffling case, and even to this day there are people who claim to know the motive and perpetrators of a baffling crime that has remained unsolved for over seventy years.

46-year-old farmer, James Dawson, had finished his game of dominos, emptied his glass and set out on the twenty-minute walk from the Edisford Bridge Hotel to his home at Bashall Hall, at Bashall Eaves, near Clitheroe. It was a little after 9 pm on Sunday, 19th March 1934, an hour before closing time, and much earlier than he usually finished his Sunday evening drink.

Halfway home, as he was approaching the entrance to Simpson's Farm, he heard the sound of a car coming up fast behind. As its headlights lit up the road ahead, he noticed what appeared to be a shadowy figure disappear into the hedgerow. When the car drove past he recognised one of the occupants as his hired help, Tom Kenyon. Dawson had asked Tom to share a drink with him that evening but he had declined, saying he had arranged to go to Clitheroe with his own friends.

Moments later, as the car disappeared out of sight, Dawson reached Simpson's Farm and as he passed the entrance he heard a gentle clicking noise. At the same time he felt a slight tap on his back, as though a small stone had struck him. He looked around, saw no one, and continued walking to the home where he lived with his

The village local, where James Dawson spent his last evening, is still a popular pub today.

three sisters and nephew. Tom Kenyon, who helped with the livestock and at the cattle auctions, also lodged on the premises.

Dawson arrived home at Bashall Hall about 9.20 pm and ate the large supper that his sister, Annie, had left on the table for him. Tom Kenyon returned at about 11 pm and after an exchange of words, possibly because he hadn't stopped to offer him a lift home, Dawson retired to bed.

Although he had suffered no pain when he felt something strike him on the back, he woke in the night to find himself in a lot of discomfort and his bedding soaked with blood. The next morning, Annie took him up a cup of tea. Examining the wound on his back she became very concerned and shouted for Kenyon, who was outside milking the cows, to come into the house

'I don't like the look of our John,' she told him, 'When I took him in his tea he asked me to look at his back where he had a bit of pain. He's covered with blood ... and there's a wound in his back!'

Dawson's chair in the kitchen where he had sat to eat his supper was also soaked as was the coat he had worn on the previous night, and there was a faint trail leading upstairs to his bedroom. Annie summoned the local doctor who persuaded John to go to hospital. Before his wound was stitched, the doctors took an X-ray of the wound and it revealed a most intriguing find.

A small egg-shaped object about the size of a man's thumbnail was lodged just under his liver, having entered through what was clearly a gaping wound above his right shoulder blade. Dawson was unwilling to have doctors operate on him. It was only when the pain became too much that on the following day he agreed to surgery to have it removed.

Examining the strange object, it was found to be a kind of home-made bullet fashioned from a short length of hard steel rod, seemingly as if it had been sawn off a poker and rounded at both ends with a file. Police officers visited Dawson in hospital and he described his journey back from the pub to his home, and how he had been struck by what he thought was a stone. It was clear now that what had caused the wound was some kind of missile, clearly fired with a great deal of force, perhaps from some sort of crossbow, catapult or airgun. Finishing his statement to the police and with his wound dressed, Dawson discharged himself and returned home.

Steadfastly maintaining that he didn't know who had, or indeed would even want to shoot him, he stubbornly refused any further medication, preferring to rest at home. However, he was persuaded to go to a nursing home in Blackburn, where on Thursday, 22nd March, he died of gangrene and septicaemia.

Assigned to the case was Detective Chief Superintendent Wilf Blacker of the West Riding Constabulary. Arriving in Bashall Eaves, a small close-knit community where everybody knew each other, it was clear from the outset that the villagers 'knew nothing'. He summoned all adults into the village hall and asked if anyone could offer any information. There was a deafening hush. Officers found

Bashall Eaves village hall where the villagers were summoned by the police to a meeting.

people crossing the street to avoid them as they carried out their enquiries, and even shopkeepers and schoolchildren fended off questions without a word. Faced with this wall of silence he examined the clues he already had.

Firstly there was Dawson's own statement that he had felt a tap on his back as he passed the farm. Secondly, this was preceded by a light clicking noise, and most importantly, the detective had in his possession the bullet that had caused the fatal wound.

Blacker summoned the London gunsmith Robert Churchill, an expert on ballistics who had assisted the police on numerous occasions. Churchill examined all local guns of any age or condition and, while this was going on, detectives made a thorough examination of sheds, garages and workshops searching for traces of the sawed-down poker used to make the bullet, or the tools that might have manufactured it.

While the hunt for evidence continued, Blacker examined other strange events that had occurred in the days since John Dawson's murder. A search of the fields beside Simpson's Farm revealed the carcass of a dog that had seemingly been shot dead. Blacker noted that although the wound seemed to have been caused by shooting, there was no sight of the bullet. Could this be the solution to the mystery? Maybe in the night darkness a poacher had mistaken the dog for a pheasant and the subsequent shot had inadvertently killed the passing farmer. It was plausible, but doubtful, as the trajectory of the bullet to hit the dog was unlikely to have caused it to hit Dawson and come to rest next to his liver.

Other strange occurrences took place within a short time. A week or so after Dawson died, Tom Kenyon and Tommy Simpson, outside whose farm the shooting had taken place, came to blows in the street. Simpson's 17-year-old daughter, Nancy had recently declared herself pregnant and refused to name the father. Although no one would speak to the police about it, detectives assumed that Simpson had accused the young farmhand of being responsible. Most mysterious of all was the sudden apparent suicide of Tommy Simpson, who hung himself in a barn less than a fortnight after Dawson's death. Despite the sudden and suspicious nature of the suicide, Blacker and his men could find nothing to suggest that it was anything more sinister.

A number of potential witnesses were asked to come forward; people who had been seen in the vicinity of the farm shortly before and after the murder. These included a broadly-built man seen carrying a walking stick, a man and woman walking a large dog, a woman wearing a green coat in the company of a young man in a trilby and, finally, a tall man wearing a trilby and fawn raincoat. But no one was talking.

The police dragged rivers and canals in and around the area as the search for a murder weapon was stepped up. It came to nothing. Churchill, the gunsmith, examined scores of guns of all types, some used for shooting game and rabbits in the local fields, others that had been brought back from the Great War and even some that had been first used when Queen Victoria was on the throne. Churchill was convinced that rather than a conventional firearm, they needed to find a self-made poacher's rifle, sometimes known as a naturalist's gun. This consisted of two barrels or tubes around two feet in length and just over an inch in diameter, and a foot pump. One of the tubes acted as a compressed air chamber and the foot pump was used to charge it. The other had two interchangeable barrels, one rifled and one smooth. The gun was assembled by screwing the tubes together, cocked in an almost clockwork fashion, using a key and loaded through a muzzle with a wad of shot.

Supporting this theory is the fact that bullets for these types of gun are often home-made. The other feature of these types of gun is the sound they make on discharge, often no more than a 'phumpff' or 'click', they are designed not to attract the attention of game keepers when used for poaching. By nature of their design, they are very easy to disguise and store and Churchill thought it likely that the murderer had already been interviewed by police but had managed to hide any trace of the gun.

An inquest was scheduled for 21st April at Blackburn and, apart from relating the events as they had been known, it was adjourned until 28th May. The second hearing was also quickly adjourned and it was finally reconvened on 25th June, again at Blackburn.

Police Surgeon Dr Gilbert Bailey stated that Dawson had received a wound to his right shoulder and that a bullet was later extracted. Death followed two days later from septicaemia. A local policeman told the inquest that he had known the deceased for several years, that he was a sober man and as far as he was aware without an enemy in the world. Summing up, the coroner said that there was no direct evidence as to how the wound was caused.

The murder remains unsolved to this day. Almost three months after it occurred, Chief Superintendent Blacker reluctantly wrote to Churchill stating: *'I am afraid I have to confess, at last, that there seems no prospect of clearing up the Bashall Eaves crime. We have done our best, and we fell short of that little bit of luck which would connect us to our man.'*

So who did kill James Dawson on that spring evening in 1934? Churchill later wrote that he felt the deceased undoubtedly knew who killed him, but didn't talk and had his own reasons for not doing so. It seems most likely he was covering up for someone. Was he scared of the repercussions if he opened his mouth?

It seems remarkable that Dawson could take such a terrific blow that it tore a hole into his shoulder and left a steel bullet in his body, then act as if nothing had happened. There is no evidence to suggest that he was sufficiently intoxicated as to not have initially felt the pain. Witnesses who saw him leave the bar stated that he was relatively sober and Tom Kenyon, who had an exchange of words with him later that night, said that Dawson wasn't drunk. Medical evidence suggested that if a bullet passes clean through a man's body it is possible for him not to realise for a time what has happened. But in this case the bullet expanded itself inside the victim. His body had to then neutralise the whole of the bullet's energy. The shock and subsequent pain he felt later that night must have been awful.

Many years later, with the case as good as written off as unsolved, Tom Kenyon said he saw a man called Harry, allegedly a relative of the Simpsons, remove a bag from the farm shortly after the shooting. Was he removing the murder weapon, or was this just another false clue that would have led to nothing? Although local rumour strongly suggests that the identity of the killer is known, no one was talking at the time and no one is talking to this day. One resident of the village spoke to a local reporter many years ago and said that his father had revealed the identity of the killer on his deathbed but had sworn him to secrecy. All he would say is that he believed Dawson had been executed for some misdemeanour.

As a postscript to this case, it is also local folklore that the ghost of James Dawson has often been seen in the area. Several witnesses have testified to seeing a ghostly figure dressed in the clothing Dawson was wearing on the night he was shot, prowling the area as if searching in vain for the evidence that could convict his killer.

And in June 2005, following appeals from relatives of the deceased, the police re-opened the case. So, will the killer finally be revealed?

SECRET WEALTH

The murder of Ruth Clarkson at Nelson, June 1936

On Monday, 22nd June 1936, Bracewell Morville walked into Nelson police station and made a statement to the effect that a dwarf was hawking jewellery around the local pubs. Two things had caused the honest citizen to be suspicious, the goods were of such a high quality they were almost certainly stolen and he had overheard the dwarf say that he had a killed a dog whilst obtaining the jewellery.

Detectives from Nelson police station decided to check out the story and made routine investigations at a number of pawnshops. They soon gathered up several objects recently sold by a dwarf, the true value of which he clearly did not appreciate. As the enquiries intensified, police suspected that they might know the origin of the jewellery.

Living at 56 Clayton Street, Nelson, was the 70-year-old spinster Ruth Clarkson, who shared her tiny terrace house with her pet fox-terrier dog, Roy. Outwardly, she lived a life of sheer poverty, with a house that perfectly fitted the picture of 1930s' depression. However, although the majority of local citizens accepted this pretence of poverty, one or two locals knew that all was not as it appeared at Clayton Street. Despite her appearance and squalid existence, Miss Clarkson was, in fact, an extremely wealthy woman, owning a few other houses in the town as well as a large amount of expensive Victorian jewellery.

Detective Superintendent Linaker and Detective Chief Inspector Fenton called at Clayton Street and knocked on the door of number

Clayton Street as it looks today. A supermarket now stands on the site where the murder took place.

56. There was no answer. Their repeated knocking alerted the attention of the next-door neighbour. She mentioned that she hadn't seen or heard anything from Ruth Clarkson for several days. More unusually, she hadn't heard the high-pitched yelp of the dog, which was very protective of its territory and should by now have been barking at the officers banging on the door.

The detectives checked around the back and found that the door showed signs of being forced, although from the condition of the house they couldn't tell if these markings were old or more recent. The neighbour told the police that Ruth's niece, Edith Edmunson lived nearby. Quickly, she was summoned to the house and admitted the officers.

The sight that greeted them was horrendous. The house was in a dreadful state: empty food tins, old newspapers, dirty bottles and plates were everywhere. Mice scurried across the floor and gnawed at scraps of food that had been left on the kitchen table. In the middle of all this, lying on the floor dressed in rags was the battered body of Ruth Clarkson. She was clearly dead: the numerous gashes on her head and upper body bore testimony to that. The murder weapon was almost certainly the blood-stained tyre lever that lay beside the body. There was blood everywhere – pools on the floor, streaks were on the walls and ceiling. But the horror didn't end there. Upstairs in the bedroom detectives were appalled to find the battered body of her pet dog suspended from the metal headboard.

Later that day, a post mortem was carried out by pathologist Dr Grace who recorded that cause of death was due to head injuries – seventeen in total, any one of which would have been fatal. The victim had a fractured skull, cheekbone and wrists, which suggested that she had desperately tried to fight off her assailant. The dog had died as a result of being strung up by a rope around its neck, after receiving a fearful kicking as it probably fought to prevent its mistress from being attacked.

The arrest of Max Mayer Haslam took less than an hour. He was not the sort of person who blended into a crowd. Bow-legged and standing at a little over four feet six inches tall, at 23-years-old he was known in the pubs and boarding houses of Nelson as 'the dwarf'.

His easily identifiable figure was spotted wandering along nearby Pendle Street, and as the darkness began to fall he was arrested on suspicion of murder and remanded in custody. He made no attempt to resist arrest but denied any knowledge of the murder of Ruth Clarkson. When asked to explain the items of jewellery in his possession, brazenly, he claimed they were his own.

With Haslam detained, an investigation into his background revealed an interesting story. He was born into a large family at Heywood, just before the First World War. He had a crippling bone disease that had left him unable to walk until he was nine, and by the time he reached his twenties his growth had been stunted and he was severely bow-legged. This disability caused him to become a surly loner and he had struggled at school. He found work in the cotton

Max Mayer Haslam known as 'The Dwarf'.

mills but when made redundant in the economic decline of the mid-1930s, he turned to a life of crime. After a number of convictions and prison terms for bungled robberies, Haslam had been released only a month before from serving a twelve-month term at Strangeways prison for theft.

Max Haslam stood trial at Manchester Assizes before Mr Justice Lawrence on 8th December 1936. He pleaded not guilty. Mr J. C. Jackson led for the Crown whilst Mr E. G. Hemmerde took charge of the defence. Evidence was shown that upon his release from gaol, Haslam had moved to Nelson where he took lodgings on Vernon Street. Here he became friendly with two unemployed labourers, James Davieson and Thomas Barlow. The three men spent their days moping around the town centre on the look out for, and plotting ways to make, some quick money.

On 13th June, Haslam's 23rd birthday, the three men went to the labour exchange and then later while walking along Scotland Road they spotted Miss Clarkson out walking her dog. Barlow spat, 'Look at that dirty old bugger, can you believe she has more money than the lot of us?' When Haslam asked how he knew that, Barlow replied that he once lived back-to-back with her and had heard a rumour that she was well off.

On 19th June, the men met up again in a town centre café. Haslam was grumbling that he was about to be evicted from his lodgings as he was struggling to find the rent money. He told his friends he was going to have a walk round the market. When they made to accompany him, he said that he was going alone and left them to finish their teas. No sooner had Haslam left the café than the two men followed him outside and watched him head towards the market. Keeping a discreet distance they saw Haslam skirt around the market and head towards Clayton Street. He then stopped outside the front door of number 56, before they decided to keep out of sight and headed back to the market. The three men met up later that evening in the Nelson Hotel and when asked if he had had any luck at the market, Haslam replied that he had not.

Haslam didn't stay at his lodgings that night but returned early the next morning. His friends noticed he seemed excited and it was soon clear that he was in possession of more money than he had been on the previous day. Later, he made a startling confession that he had killed a dog during a robbery. As he made more revelations during the day, it became clear that he had in all probability returned to Clayton Street the night before and carried out the attack. The two friends decided to make statements about their suspicions to the police, unaware that by that time Haslam was already under arrest.

The defence suggested that the two 'friends' were responsible for the crime and they had concocted an alibi for the purpose of framing their erstwhile colleague.

The prosecution called a witness who testified that he had sold the tyre lever found at the scene of the crime to Haslam two days before the murder and another witness, who saw Haslam drop an item down a drain on Leeds Road. Police lifted the grid and recovered a watchcase that was found to have belonged to Miss Clarkson.

In the face of a wealth of evidence, including Haslam's weak alibi that he was at a cricket match when the crime was committed, the three-day trial ended in the only possible verdict, the jury deliberated for just less than an hour before finding him guilty. His appeal in January was dismissed and he was returned to Strangeways to await execution.

Haslam was due to be hanged alongside George Royle, a Stockport man who had killed a woman in the 'East Lancs Road Murder', but just hours before the scheduled double execution Royle was reprieved and Haslam alone faced hangmen Tom and Albert Pierrepoint. His brother waited outside the prison in tears for the notice of execution to be posted, telling a reporter that his father had refused to see Haslam while awaiting execution and had said that if the authorities hadn't have hanged him he would have done it himself!

THE UNSEEING EYES OF THE LAW

The murder of Ella Staunton at Liverpool, May 1946

Liverpool City Police had long suspected that Mrs Ella Valentine Staunton, the 41-year-old proprietress of 'Bobby's Gentleman's Manicurist Saloon' was offering customers a little more than just a manicure in her basement salon. Indeed, six years before, in the early part of 1940, they had on file evidence that Mrs Staunton and her then partner, Gladys Henderson, were running a brothel from similar premises in Rumford Street. But whilst evidence was still being compiled, Mrs Henderson had been killed in an air raid. Police decided not to proceed with the investigation, but kept the file open.

On Monday afternoon, 20th May 1946, two plain-clothed detectives took up their positions in a small engineering workshop and waited. A piece of floor board had been lifted and from their vantage point, Constables Anderson and Ballam were able to spy through a ventilator grill on the comings and goings below at 'Bobby's', in the basement at 7a Tempest Hey, Liverpool.

Surveillance at the premises had been ordered following a tip-off to the Liverpool police that there were 'bawdy goings on' at the salon. It was part of a long running on-and-off investigation and nearly six years later police had decided to see if there was a case worth answering. The surveillance was set up in early spring. Due to other duties, the watch had been scaled down recently and it was after a fortnight's gap that the police returned to Tempest Hey to resume the enquiry.

The constables had arrived at the premises at 4.15 pm, and already they could hear voices from down below. Such was their vantage point that they could see only one of the booths and part of the lounge area of the manicure salon, but this was were Ella Staunton sat the customer as she offered him a drink. Their view of the situation was lessened when Mrs Staunton directed the customer into a different booth. When she followed carrying a basin of water and towels, they assumed that everything was above board and the customer was indeed there for legitimate reasons.

After a few minutes, the man left the booth only to return a moment later. This time, however the officers heard sounds of a struggle taking place. Constable Ballam turned to his colleague: 'It sounds like he's giving her a good hiding, we'd better check this out.' The two officers rushed to the connecting staircase and descended. They knocked on the door and, receiving no reply, crossed the street to Exchange Station and telephoned the salon. The phone was engaged so they returned just as a man was leaving the building. Before they could speak he closed the door behind him and headed for the street.

The two officers approached and making themselves known, asked the man for some identification. He withdrew his National Health card bearing the name Thomas Hendren, with an address in Birkenhead. Constable Anderson again knocked at the door only for Hendren to tell him he was wasting his time.

'There's a man in there, she won't answer for a quarter of an hour or twenty minutes. You know what Ella is, she's a prostitute.'

Hendren then said that he was in a hurry to get back to Birkenhead and, after making a note of his details, he was allowed to leave.

After waiting ten or so minutes, Ballam again telephoned the salon. Still he got the engaged tone. Both officers then returned and began to knock loudly on the door, shouting that they were police officers. They listened closely but could hear no sound, and it was then that they finally decided to force an entry.

Walking down the narrow passage they noticed that the carpet was ruffled up and in the entrance to the lounge at the side they saw a pair of women's shoes. A large standard lamp lit up the lounge and on the floor just inside the doorway was the body of Ella Staunton. She was lying on her back, her head covered in blood and a piece of lighting flex tied around her neck. Splashes of blood were visible on the walls and carpet. She had been the victim of a vicious attack and a blood-stained case opener, resembling a small pickaxe, was found in the kitchen area.

Realising that the woman was beyond help, Anderson stood guard as Ballam went upstairs to telephone for an ambulance and inform his superiors.

Under the direction of Superintendent Smith, Chief Inspector Anthony Hall of Liverpool CID took charge of the investigation. He was joined at the scene later that evening by pathologist Dr William Henry Grace of Liverpool University Hospital and Dr James Firth from the North West Forensic Science Laboratory at Preston. A post-mortem was carried out that night. Although it had been assumed that death was due to wounds caused by the case opener or strangulation, when the body was stripped they found that death had, in fact, been due to a wound to the heart, probably caused by a knife.

In her youth, Ella Valentine French had been a beautiful young woman. Slim and with long flowing red hair, she had worked as a dancer and manicurist and travelled the world before marrying Thomas Staunton of Crosby, in 1934. She had had a child from a previous relationship but none from the marriage, which lasted four years. They had been apart for almost eight years, and for a time she had been living with a Dutch naval officer until he was killed in action. Suspicions that she was a prostitute were met with some disbelief by relatives, shocked at the terrible tragedy.

Enquiries into Thomas Hendren, the man seen leaving the salon shortly before the murder was discovered, found that although he had given his address as Roe Street, Birkenhead, he hadn't been seen there since a family argument eleven days earlier. A wanted notice was issued and a manhunt set up.

Hendren, it was learnt, was a 31-year-old unemployed ship's baker who police had had in custody on 3rd May, charged with theft from Hubbard and Martins, his employers at Birkenhead. Hendren had

WANTED FOR INTERVIEW BY LIVERPOOL POLICE IN CONNECTION WITH THE
MURDER OF A WOMAN ON 20TH INST.,

THOMAS HENDREN

31 YEARS, OCCUPATION BAKER OR SHIP'S BAKER,   5 FT 9", WELL SET UP

SHOULDERS, SMALL FACE AND THIN FEATURES, CLEAN SHAVEN, BROWN EYES, FAIR HAIR,

THIN ON TOP, DRESSED IN A BROWN CHECK SUIT, BROWN TRILBY HAT, BLACK SHOES.

IS IN POSSESSION OF A KNIFE DESCRIBED AS A LARGE MEXICAN TYPE POCKET

KNIFE WITH A MOTTLED HANDLE.

PHOTOGRAPH HEREWITH.   TAKEN ABOUT TEN YEARS AGO.

ANY INFORMATION PLEASE TELEPHONE CENTRAL 6666 OR INFORM ANY POLICE

OFFICER.

CRIMINAL INVESTIGATION DEPARTMENT.

LIVERPOOL.

The 'wanted' poster that was issued by the Liverpool police.

been accused of stealing property from the factory, which he had subsequently sold in pubs in the area. He was awaiting further charges as a result of this and he had left home after his mother found he had prised open a savings box in his sister's room and stolen money and saving certificates. Told that if he didn't return them that day his sister would press charges, and mindful of the other charges pending, he had decided to flee.

His mother told police that Hendren had been well-behaved and law abiding until he had left his last ship in January 1945 through illness and, although he had held a few jobs since then, he was unable to settle and usually dismissed after a few days. His whole demeanour had changed when his fiancée, Marjorie McLeary, who worked at a post office in Salford, broke off their engagement.

Since she had ended their relationship in the spring of 1945, possibly after Hendren had infected her with venereal disease, he had become severely depressed. This culminated in June when his mother found him with his head in the gas oven. Hendren had also swallowed a large number of aspirin the day before. Both efforts to end his life failed and he was subsequently sent to prison for attempted suicide.

Released from Walton in June 1945, he had been out of work and under medical supervision until he found work at Martin and Hubbards, which lasted until he was dismissed for theft. Marjorie also told the police that Hendren was in possession of a wicked looking nine-inch knife which he said had been given to him by a Mexican during one of his voyages.

The hunt for Thomas Hendren brought several leads. A taxi driver told police he had picked up a man matching Hendren's description at the Ocean Club on Lord Street, at around 5 pm that Monday. The caller had said on the phone he wanted a taxi to Birkenhead but had then asked to be driven to Huyton station. The journey to Huyton was made via Wavertree, after the driver was informed the passenger wanted to buy a raincoat. Told that he would have been better buying one in the city centre, the man said he wanted to purchase a second-hand one, but after failing to do so he called into a Wavertree gent's outfitters where he purchased a cheap 'mac'. He left clothing coupons which were later found to bear the name Staunton.

The hunt took police to Huyton where the trail petered out. On the following day, Hendren telephoned his sister in Llandudno. Police had already spoken to her and the call was traced to St Helens, but by the time officers reached the call box Hendren had disappeared. The handset from the call box was fingerprinted and removed as evidence.

On the following morning, a porter at Huyton railway station found a number of papers stashed behind the toilet bowl, including an identity card belonging to Hendren, confirming that he had indeed been the passenger in the taxi.

Hendren was eventually picked up by detectives in Salford on the Thursday morning. Warned that he might try to visit his former fiancée, officers in Salford were furnished with a description of the wanted man, and at 6 am that morning Sgt Vaughan and PC Ward of Salford City Police entered a public toilet block in Albert Park and found a man sitting in a cubicle. Asked for his name, he said he was called McLeary and that he was going home after spending the night with a woman. Asked again, he said that he was called Johnston, but was unable to prove his identity.

'I believe your name is not Johnston but Thomas Hendren,' the Sergeant told him.

'Yes Sergeant, they want me for Ella,' Hendren said.

He was searched and found to be in possession of several items bearing the name Ella Staunton, including a lighter, fountain pen and wallet.

'I took these out of her handbag after I had done her with the case-opener,' he said after being placed under arrest. Up until that time no mention had been made in the press about a case-opener.

Three hours later, Hendren was questioned by officers from Liverpool and made two short statements before he was returned to Liverpool.

'All I want to say is that I did it,' Hendren said in his first statement after being cautioned. He further elaborated on the journey back:

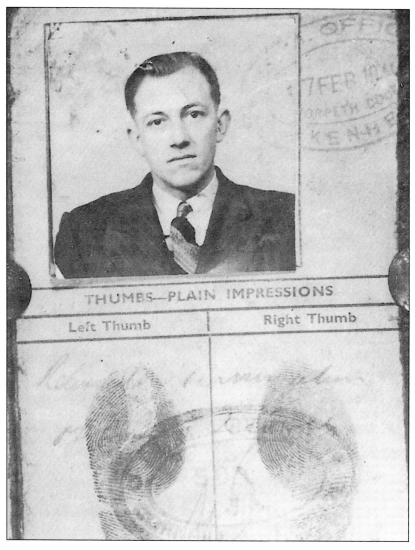

Thomas Hendren's identity card was found stashed at Huyton railway station.

'She's had plenty out of me, over a £100 in the five years I've known her and when I asked her to lend me a couple of quid she wouldn't so it happened. I got about £10 out of her handbag, a £5 note and five £1s ... I bought a case-opener in Lewis's that morning. I thought of breaking in somewhere.'

The background into the sordid case was revealed when Hendren stood trial at Liverpool Assizes, before Mr Justice Oliver on Thursday, 27th June 1946. Mr Basil Nield KC and Mr Leslie Rigg represented Hendren, while Mr H I Nelson KC and Mr Robertson-Crichton led for the Crown.

The Crown's case was simply that Hendren had murdered Ella Staunton. By his confession, Hendren had claimed that he had been a client and frequent visitor at 'Bobby's Salon', and he had killed Mrs Staunton after she had refused to loan him a sum of money. After carrying out the vicious attack he had then stolen almost £20 which he had all but spent when he was picked up after travelling to Salford, where his former fiancée lived.

Although the evidence against Hendren was conclusive, the case was far from a formality. The defence chose not to contest any of the police evidence, instead they based their case on the issue of insanity.

Once the Crown had finished presenting their case, Mr Nield took the stand and told the jury that his answer to the charge was that at the time of the incident Thomas Hendren was insane. He called members of the family as witnesses to show that Hendren had a 'flaring temper' and his love of comic books showed his immaturity.

Evidence was also heard of a traumatic time which the accused had endured whilst serving in the Merchant Navy in Singapore. His ship was one of the last to leave and he had been given the duty of going ashore to help bury some of the dead. It was alleged that due to the numbers of bodies it had been impossible to bury them and as a result they had had to be piled into human bonfires, petrol poured onto them then set alight. The smell was sickening and Hendren had told his family that it had been a horrible experience.

It seemed that all aspects of his insanity stemmed from after this period. It was brought up how in 1945, on the day before he tried to gas himself he had taken 120 aspirin tablets in an unsuccessful attempt at suicide.

The prosecution challenged the insanity evidence when they asked the jury to consider that after committing the murder, Hendren had purchased a raincoat to cover the bloodstains on his suit. Medical officers who had examined Hendren during the period leading to the trial were called and none could confirm that he was insane. The closest the defence got from this line of enquiry was when Dr Grace admitted that by putting his head in a gas oven Hendren might be showing signs of insanity. Although pressed further, Dr Grace couldn't be led to make an opinion on other events after this time.

Summing up the evidence on the second and last day of the trial, the judge asked the jury to consider if they believed that Hendren knew what he was doing at the time of the murder and that if he did, did he know he was doing wrong. He pointed out that the accused had purchased the murder weapon on that day, and that after brutally attacking the woman because she had refused to lend him a sum of money, he stole from her and fled the area.

After a short consideration, the jury returned to find him guilty as charged. There was no appeal on behalf of Hendren; instead hopes were pinned on the sentence being commuted. It was not to be and on Wednesday, 17th July 1946, Thomas Hendren was hanged at Walton Gaol, Liverpool, by Albert Pierrepoint and Herbert Morris.

Somewhat surprisingly, the two officers who had been observing the salon on the afternoon of the murder were put up for commendation. The reason for this was that their diligence in taking Hendren's name had saved police a great deal of work in tracing a suspect. How they failed to spot the bloodstains on Hendren's suit, and for which he had had to purchase a raincoat to cover, was never explained. The commendation was later rejected.

THE FYLDE HAG

---✿---

The witch's grave at Woodplumpton

St Anne's church lies at the centre of a large, rural parish covering Woodplumpton, Upper and Lower Bartle, Catforth and Cottom, in the Fylde area of north Lancashire. St Anne's church is also the final resting place of a mysterious lady who, 300 years ago, roamed the moors between Preston and Blackpool spreading mischief and fear. Legend goes that fearful of her return after death, the locals placed a large stone over her grave. This boulder, about three foot by two foot, still lies beside the path in the churchyard and is marked to this day with a small plaque, proclaiming that here is the grave of Meg Shelton – a local witch.

Marjorie 'Meg' Shelton, the Fylde Witch, or the Hag of Fylde, lived at Catforth in the late 17th century. She is said to have plagued the area and there are a number of tales about her strange behaviour. One story tells of a local farmer who, one evening late in the summer, caught her stealing corn from his barn. The farmer made a deal with Meg. He told her he would set his greyhound on her. If she could outrun the dog to her cottage in Catforth she could stay, but if she failed she must leave the area. Meg Shelton reached the threshold of the cottage with the hound hot on her trail, so close in fact that the dog was able to sink its teeth into her heel as it chased her through the door. The 'race' was decided a dead heat. Meg stayed in the cottage but, from that day, she walked with a limp.

Meg Shelton was alleged to have got up to all sorts of mischief. She is said to have stolen the milk from cattle and transformed herself into animals, her favourite being a small white cat. She was said to be

The grave of Meg Shelton in St Anne's churchyard.

able to change into different shapes as a form of disguise. One farmer near Kirkham, spied Meg Shelton entering his barn to steal grain. He knew she could only leave the barn the way she had entered. So he picked up his pitchfork and followed her, only to find himself facing his rows of sacks, but no Meg. Deciding she must have concealed herself inside a sack he took to thrusting his pitchfork into each in turn. As he jabbed at the last bag in the line, it made a blood-curdling scream and instantly turned back into Meg Shelton!

Meg Shelton died in 1705: she was crushed to death when a barrel fell on her, although rumour has it that she was buried alive. It is also said that sometimes her grave appears to have been disturbed and that she has been seen walking across the fields.

As these sightings and disturbances at the grave became more common it was decided to take action. A Cottam priest was called to perform an exorcism and Meg's body was re-interred in a narrow shaft, dug as for a fence post. To prevent her scratching her way out, she was placed in headfirst so that, if she did try to dig her way out, she'd be going the wrong way! A large stone was then placed on top of the grave. She did not get out again. Or did she?

In the winter of 1933, a schoolboy ran terrified from the church having seen 'an old woman dressed in funny clothes'. Others have also claimed to have seen a small white cat walking near the grave.

The grave is still there today and is also the setting of a curious ritual, invented it is claimed to both ward off evil spirits and grant a wish to those brave or silly enough to carry it out. Handed down through generations the custom is that when there is a full moon, one must walk around the grave three times and stand on the stone. You then first look to the north, the east, the south and then finally to the west. Then your wish will come true.

HANGED FOR THE WRONG CRIME?

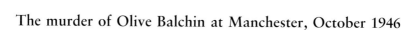

The murder of Olive Balchin at Manchester, October 1946

It was almost closing time at the small pawnbroker shop at 3 Downing Street in the Manchester suburb of Ardwick, when a man walked in and asked to buy the hammer on display in the shop window. Having only just purchased the hammer in a collection of tools that afternoon, the manager, Edward Macdonald, thought it was probably not the most suitable of the ones he had for sale. Flat faced and with a softer than normal head, it was the type of hammer used by leather workers. It was made all the more memorable by the fact that the previous owner had replaced the wooden shaft and somewhat botched the job.

Enquiring on what the man planned to use it for, he was told that it was for general purpose.

'Well, that's really not going to be much use,' he told the customer, adding that it wasn't even suitable for knocking in a nail.

'It will suit my purposes,' the man replied and handing over the three shillings and sixpence, he placed it into his raincoat pocket, bid the manager goodnight and walked away in the direction of the town centre.

On Sunday morning, 20th October 1946, James Acarnley was making his way across the bomb site at the junction of Deansgate and Cumberland Street when he saw two young boys trying to attract his attention. Their waving and shouting caused him to cross over to where they pointed to the body of a woman, lying in the

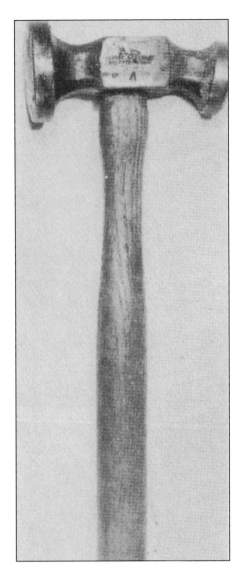

The murder weapon.

undergrowth close to a wall. He summoned the police and Sergeant Thomas Ross hurried from nearby Bootle Street station to what was at once identified as a murder scene. Dr Charles Jenkins was called and was able to ascertain that it was the body of a woman, aged around mid to late thirties and that the most likely cause of death was as a result of the numerous lacerations to the head and face.

Detective Inspector Frank Stainton was placed in charge of the murder. The first task was to make a search of the bomb site. The police found three vital clues: a bloodstained hammer, along with some crepe wrapping paper shaped as if it had been around a hammer, and an identity card which gave the woman's name as Olive Balchin, a known prostitute.

Investigations in the Deansgate area brought forward a number of witnesses. Norman Mercer, landlord of the Dog and Partridge, told

Olive Balchin's body was discovered lying on an old bomb site.

police that he had been out walking his dog at midnight when he saw a man and woman arguing close to where the body was subsequently discovered. He was able to make a detailed description of the man: dark hair, fresh complexion with a dark suit and light raincoat. When taken to the mortuary, he was also able to identify the body as that of the woman he had seen the previous evening.

Later that week, seeing a picture of the murder weapon in the evening paper, Edward MacDonald was able to tell detectives that he had sold a hammer similar to the murder weapon on the previous Saturday. He was also able to give detectives a thorough description of the customer, which was very close to the one given by Mercer.

On the following day, Elizabeth Copley a waitress at the Queens Café near Deansgate, came forward and told the police that she had seen two women and a man in her café between 10 pm and 11 pm on the Saturday night. The younger woman she recognised as a frequent customer whom she knew as Olive 'Balshaw'. The man was described as wearing a light coloured raincoat and was carrying a parcel wrapped in brown paper.

Although they had a good description of the wanted man, he didn't match any known offenders in the area. As a result, officers on the case made the usual round of beat enquiries calling at houses, cafés, shops and pubs in the city centre, as well as lodging houses and hostels.

While these enquiries were going on, a complaint was made by a lodger at a Services' transit dormitory, who reported that a man named Roland had taken his raincoat and failed to return it. As a number of the witnesses had mentioned the man they were seeking was wearing a light raincoat, the same colour as the one missing from the hostel, Sergeant Emrys Trippier was sent to make enquiries.

Although there was no one on record with the name Roland, it was soon clear that the man in question was Walter Graham Rowland, a man with a long string of convictions dating back to the 1920s, and who, in 1934, had been convicted of murder. When a check on Olive's clients also revealed the name of Walter Rowland, he now became prime suspect.

On 26th October, Detective Sergeant Blakemore and Constable

Walter Graham Rowland.

Nimmo were sent to pick up Rowland at the Services' transit dormitory. Nimmo knew Rowland from a previous offence of breaking into a warehouse, for which he was currently still on probation. Aware of the complaint made by his fellow lodger he assumed that he was being picked up in connection with the missing raincoat. Back at the station he was questioned about the murder case and admitted knowing Olive Balchin. He then provided the police with a possible motive. Rowland presented officers with a card showing he was being treated for venereal disease, which he believed he might have picked up from Olive. He then made the damning statement that he would have strangled her if she had infected him.

Although all leads so far led to Rowland, he was able to furnish detectives with an alibi. He claimed that at 8.15 on the night of the murder he had visited his mother, Mrs Agnes Hall, at her home in New Mills, Derbyshire, remaining until 9.20, when he caught the bus to Manchester. The bus took him as far as Stockport from where he needed to catch a connection. Rowland claimed he was then in the Wellington public house until late, and Sergeant Jones of the Stockport Police backed up his story. Rowland was unsure of the exact times he had been in the pub but remembered two policemen enter the bar, make a quick check and then leave. Sergeant Jones later testified that he and a constable had been in the pub at 10.30.

Leaving the pub, Rowland caught a bus back to Manchester and arriving back at Ardwick he went to a chip shop before booking into a lodging house at 81 Brunswick Street. He signed the register at about 11 pm and, after popping out for ten minutes to try to buy some mineral water, he said he had returned and gone to bed. The landlord of the lodging house agreed with Rowland's timing and produced the register as evidence. Therefore the alibi was that at the time of the murder Rowland was in bed in Ardwick, two or three miles from the murder site.

Rowland had mentioned he believed that Olive Balchin, who he admitted to having sex with on more than one occasion, had given him VD. A post mortem, which had confirmed the cause of death as due to savage head injuries, found no trace of sexually transmitted diseases in the dead woman.

At an identity parade held a week after the body was found, both Elizabeth Copley and Edward Macdonald picked out Rowland. Later that afternoon he was charged with the murder of Olive Balchin. He said he was not guilty. At another parade held the following week he was identified by Norman Mercer.

Charged with the wilful murder of Olive Balchin, Walter Rowland stood trial before Mr Justice Sellers at Manchester Assizes in mid-December. His alibi was to form the bulk of the defence, but the jury was told it would hear evidence to contradict the alibi.

The three witnesses who had identified Rowland as the purchaser of the hammer, and of being in the area at the time of the murder could not be shaken under examination. There were flaws in Rowland's defence: firstly, on examining the register at the Ardwick hotel where allegedly he had stayed the night of the murder, detectives noticed that the checkout date was 19th October, not the 20th as he had claimed. Rowland's defence stated that this was an input error by the owner. Other entries in the book showed that the logging of dates and times of guests was erratic. Nevertheless, it was a fact that went towards showing his alibi wasn't concrete.

Although the owner of the hotel testified that Rowland was in his room from 11.30 pm, he could not swear that Rowland could not have feasibly left the house. Rowland would probably have had to make certain he could get back in without being spotted, which the owner said was most unlikely.

The evidence against Rowland comprised mainly the identification by the key witnesses, who separately named Rowland as the man who purchased the hammer, was in the company of the murdered woman on the night of the murder and was seen quarrelling with a woman close to the murder scene.

Forensic evidence found traces of dirt identical to that on the bomb site in the turn-ups of Rowland's trousers. There were traces of blood on his shoe, however they were too small to be grouped. This point was pounced on by the defence, who pointed out that the brutal nature of the assault was such that the killer would surely have had traces of blood on his clothing. There was none found on any of the clothes in Rowland's possession.

On the fourth day of the trial the judge summed up the evidence and invited the jury to seek a verdict. They took less than two hours to find Rowland guilty of murder and for the second time in his life he stood and heard the judge pass sentence of death on him.

Once sentence had been passed, the jury were informed that in 1934 Rowland had been convicted of the murder of his young daughter. He had been sentenced to death and was taken to Strangeways gaol to await execution, scheduled for 14th June 1934. However, just forty-eight hours before he was due to hang, Rowland was reprieved and went on to serve eight years, being released in June 1942 on condition that he joined the armed forces. He was demobbed in 1945 and since then had lodged and worked in Manchester, mixing with criminals and prostitutes and sending his washing home to his mother in New Mills.

Rowland was once more taken to Strangeways gaol and occupied the same cell that he had vacated over twelve years before. He launched an appeal and a hearing was set for 27th January 1947.

On 22nd January, the governor of Walton Gaol, Liverpool, received a note from one of his prisoners. David Ware was serving a short sentence after confessing to a theft from a Salvation Army hostel in Stoke.

Ware told the governor that it was he who had committed the murder of Olive Balchin at Manchester and that Rowland was not guilty. Once news of this was relayed to Manchester, detectives travelled to Liverpool to interview Ware. Two days later he made a detailed confession to the police in which he claimed to have killed Olive Balchin shortly before 10 pm on the night of 19th October 1946.

When Rowland's appeal took place on 27th January, they asked for the verdict to be quashed, based on the testimony of Ware. After considering the request in light of the new information received, an application for an adjournment of fourteen days was granted. Two days later, Ware was interviewed at length by Rowland's legal team, to whom he repeated his confession of murder.

On 10th February, Rowland's appeal took place at the Central

David Ware.

Criminal Court. The request to hear the evidence of David Ware was refused, although two new witnesses were allowed to give evidence, neither of whom could do more than place Rowland in Stockport on the evening of the murder.

As Lord Goddard dismissed the appeal, Rowland made a passionate speech from the dock: '... I am an innocent man. This is the greatest injustice which has ever happened in an English court. Why did you have the man who confessed here today and not hear him? I am not allowed justice because of my past!'

As Lord Goddard ordered Rowland be taken down he continued his plea: 'It would have knocked the bottom out of English Law to have acquitted me and proved my innocence. I say now I am an innocent man before God.'

A week later, with a new date set for execution, the Home Secretary ordered an inquiry. After a detailed analysis of all the evidence heard at the trial and new evidence that wasn't heard, it came to the conclusion that Ware's confession was false, that he had been wrong about the time of the murder and had seemingly just pieced together his confession from newspaper reports.

On 22nd February, David Ware withdrew his confession and, on 27th February, Rowland was hanged at Strangeways by Albert Pierrepoint and Henry Critchell. He left two letters in the condemned cell, written at dawn as he waited to die. The first was to his parents reiterating his pleas of innocence. In the other letter to his solicitor he wrote that he hoped he would carry on trying to clear his name for a crime he swore he did not commit.

On 10th July 1951, with Walter Rowland in his grave and the campaign for his conviction to be quashed a mere memory, David John Ware tried to batter a woman to death in Bristol. He had bought himself a new hammer with which to commit the crime. Tried on 16th November, he was found guilty but insane and committed to Broadmoor where he hanged himself in his cell on 1st April 1954. Despite these events, Rowland's case was never reviewed and there are still people who believe that Walter Graham Rowland was reprieved for a murder he did commit and hanged for one he did not.

THE BLACKBURN
FINGERPRINT HUNT

The Murder of June Anne Devaney at Blackburn, May 1948

Just a month short of her fourth birthday, June Anne Devaney was last seen sleeping peacefully in her hospital cot, shortly before midnight. Just over an hour later, Nurse Gwendoline Humphries noticed a draught blowing through the ward and the young child's cot was empty. The nurse also noticed something else that was amiss. Standing at the foot of the cot was a glass Winchester bottle used to hold distilled water, usually kept on a trolley in the ward. A trail of large, adult footprints made with what looked like bare feet led across the highly polished floor.

June, a patient in CH3 ward of Blackburn's Queen's Park Hospital had been admitted ten days earlier suffering from pneumonia. She had made a good recovery and was due to be discharged later that day. When she was discovered missing a search of the ward and adjacent bathrooms soon escalated into a full-scale search involving the local police. At 3.17 am, PC Edward Parkinson made the gruesome discovery when he spotted the young girl's body lying face down in the grass, less than a hundred yards from the ward and close to the perimeter fence. Whilst detectives from Scotland Yard hurried to Blackburn, the police surgeon reported that she had been killed with appalling brutality. She had severe injuries caused by a vicious sexual assault, but death had occurred as a result of the killer swinging her by her feet and smashing her head against a wall. There were also bruises to her neck and bite marks to her chest. The

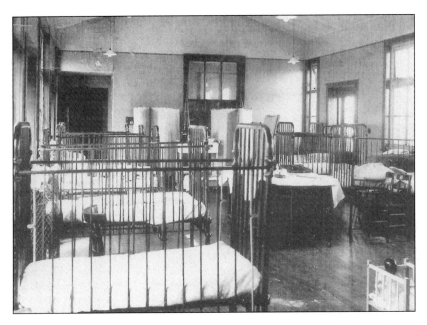

The hospital ward where June was admitted, suffering from pneumonia.

Scotland Yard detectives who helped track down the murderer both later commented that the scene of crime photographs were the most horrifying they had ever seen.

Detectives soon believed that the killer was likely to be a local man. Entrance to the hospital grounds seemed to have been made via a gap in a wooden fence, accessed by a narrow footpath along the side of a steep-sided, disused quarry known locally as a delph, which led to Queen's Road. It was the sort of short cut that locals would use, certainly not the kind a stranger would be aware of, especially in the darkness.

A local taxi driver added weight to this theory when he came forward to say he had dropped off a man outside the hospital, close to the spot where the killer had entered the grounds. After collecting his

A policeman guards the spot where the body was found.

fare the driver watched as the man made his way towards the quarry and in the direction of the hospital. He couldn't give detectives a description but did recall that he spoke in a broad, Lancastrian accent.

Quickly the clues began to mount. The most vital was a set of fingerprints found on the Winchester bottle beside the cot. There were well over a dozen sets of prints on the heavy bottle, some fresh, many having been there for weeks, even months. Nevertheless, once prints were taken of all those with genuine reason to handle the sterile water container, it left one crisp, clear set of prints unaccounted for and belonging more likely than not to the killer. These prints had been left by someone with large hands. Taking this into consideration, along with photographs taken of the footprint trail in the ward, it was suggested that the killer was around six foot tall.

The police already thought they had a suspect. When asked if they had noticed anything suspicious, nurses mentioned that a man had been seen in the grounds a few days earlier, and on one occasion had been spotted peering intently through a window at the nurses' quarters, close to the Children's Ward. A few days later he was spotted in the hospital and arrested by detectives. Under questioning, it was learned that the man had been to the hospital visiting relatives. While he later admitted to spying on the nurses, he strenuously denied any involvement in the murder. His footprints and fingerprints were taken and although they didn't match those at the hospital, he was cautioned and warned to keep away from the hospital.

Sifting through the evidence, DCI Jack Capstick, the officer in charge of the investigation, came to a number of conclusions. Everything kept coming back to the prints on the Winchester bottle. As they didn't match any already on file, this suggested that the killer did not have a criminal record. Also, they were clearly those of a younger person, not worn and disfigured, as one would expect from an older man, with perhaps decades of hard manual labour in mills, mines or factories. Therefore if the killer was young, it was a possibility that he was a serviceman, someone who had perhaps returned to his unit having been in Blackburn at the time of the murder. Detectives also considered that the violent nature of the crime suggested that the killer might have struck before, although perhaps not in this country. Urgent enquiries were sent to all places where the forces were stationed across Europe and beyond, hoping the matching print might be found.

With alarming newspaper headlines, questioning whether the murder was the work of a serial killer and referring to the unsolved crimes of young children in nearby Bolton in recent months, Chief Constable Looms, head of Lancashire CID, made a dramatic announcement four days after the murder. He said it was decided to fingerprint every male over the age of sixteen who had been in Blackburn on the night of 14th May. It was a mammoth task, one which had never been attempted on such a scale before. The Mayor of Blackburn started off the appeal by offering to become the first volunteer. With reassurances that the prints would be destroyed once they had been eliminated, the job got underway. Dividing each of the town's fourteen voting wards into zones, officers used the Electoral Register to make out a list, alphabetically listing the streets and

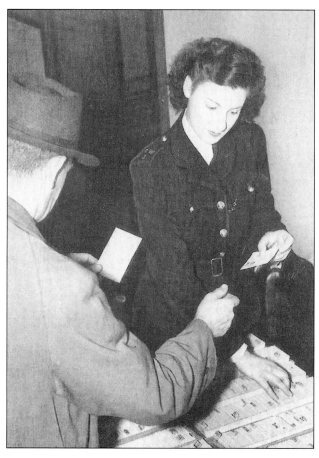

A huge police operation was mounted to fingerprint every male who had been in Blackburn on the night of 14th May.

cross-referencing it with the occupants. There were over 120,000 residents in Blackburn in over 35,000 homes and, although many of the men were still displaced by the armed forces, detectives had to produce over 46,000 cards to collect the print samples.

Measuring a little over three inches square, the card was designed to take the impression of the left forefinger and thumb on the front. This would be recorded next to details of the person's name, age, address and national registration number. On the reverse were the prints of the four fingers from the left hand.

Dubbed 'Operation Fingerprint' in the press, the campaign kicked off on Sunday, 23rd May when, armed with a batch of cards and little black inking pads, the kind used with rubber stamps, officers began house-to-house enquiries. Each afternoon the latest batch of prints was sent to Preston for specialist examination.

Fingerprinting was not simply a case of comparison, moreover it was an exact science. At the turn of the century Sir Edward Henry, Commissioner of Scotland Yard, had come up with a way of classifying prints based on the ridges of the fingers falling into four types: whorls, loops, arches or a combination of all three. By giving each part of the finger a number, written as a fraction in accordance to its place on the finger, this was then added to the other numbers on that finger to give it a comparison figure. With 1,024 different groups, this narrowed down the number of prints that needed a more detailed examination, and saved many, many man-hours.

For the next ten weeks officers worked a twelve-hour day taking prints and sending them away for examination. By the end of July, the Electoral Register was completed and every print taken had been checked and eliminated. At the end of June, a new set of ration books was issued mainly to returning servicemen, a number of whom were not listed on the registers used in the first checks. With the town closed for the traditional fortnight holiday, officers suspended the fingerprinting and concentrated on cross-checking the new ration card issues with the Electoral Register.

As the town got back to work after the holidays, it was learnt that there were just over 900 names that needed to be checked. A new plan was drawn up and on Monday, 9th August, officers went to

Peter Griffiths.

collect the next batch of prints. On the Thursday afternoon, as the latest batch of prints was being examined, they finally got the break through.

Card number 46235 had been taken on the previous afternoon. It bore the name Peter Griffiths, aged 22, of 31 Birley Street, Blackburn and carried the registration number NBA 6917-188. It belonged, as long suspected, to an ex-serviceman and was one of the last batch generated. The card bore an identical thumb and left forefinger print as those found at the scene of the murder.

Griffiths was a tall, ex Welsh-Guardsman, who worked as a flour packer in a local mill. Where the Griffiths family lived, common amongst terraced houses, was one continuous loft running the length of the street. It was therefore decided to make the arrest outside the house, to prevent the suspect trying to make an escape through the roof space. Officers waited in cars at both ends of the street for a number of hours before the suspect came into sight. At just before 9 pm on Friday, 13th August, as Griffith approached his front door, he was stopped in the street and placed under arrest.

Initially denying any involvement with the murder or ever being near the hospital, he later admitted on the journey to the police station that he used to play in the delph. Cautioned that anything he said might be used in evidence, Griffiths asked if he had been arrested because of his fingerprints. When he was told that it was, he stopped for a moment then said, 'Well, if they are my fingerprints on the bottle I will tell you all about it.'

What he said next formed the basis of the prosecution case when he stood trial for murder before Mr Justice Oliver on 15th October 1948, at Lancaster Assizes.

Griffiths' version of events was that he had left his house at about 6 pm and gone to the Dun Horse pub where he downed five pints of beer. He then went to Yates Wine Lodge where he drank Guinness and rum before returning to the Dun Horse for another half dozen pints of bitter. He left on his own and made his way towards Darwen Road where he got into conversation with a man after asking for a cigarette light. After chatting for around fifteen minutes the man offered him a lift home, but Griffiths said he didn't want to go home yet as he planned to go for a walk to sober up a little. He was given a lift in the car and dropped off close to the hospital gates.

According to the accused, he couldn't recall climbing the railing but the next thing he remembered was standing outside the children's ward.

'I left my shoes at the door ... I just went in and heard a nurse humming ... I waited a few minutes ... Then I went back in again ... I picked up a biggish bottle ...'

Griffiths went on to say how he had stumbled against a cot as he heard a nurse approach and this had caused the child to wake up. She opened her eyes and started to cry, whereupon Griffith picked her up to try to quieten her down. Still carrying her in his arms, he made his way out into the grounds.

'I walked with her down the hospital field. I put her down on the grass. She started crying again and I tried to stop her ... she wouldn't stop crying and I just lost my temper, and then you know what happened ... I banged her head against the wall then went back to put my shoes on ... I then went back to where the child was. I just glanced at her ... then went straight down the field to the delph.'

He then said he had gone home and as his parents where asleep he had slept on the sofa. His behaviour on the following day gave no cause for concern to his parents, and he had aroused no suspicion in anyone in the weeks leading up to his arrest.

Faced with the prisoner's confession, his defence chose the only option open to them: to plead that the accused was insane at the time of the crime. Mr Basil Neild KC brought in evidence that Griffiths had a history of mental illness and his father had been an inmate in Prestwich Asylum. His mother testified that as a child he had fallen off a milk float and banged his head. Following this accident he was prone to blackouts. Medical evidence was also offered to suggest that Griffiths was a schizophrenic, but it was a hopeless case.

The Crown's case was strong. Mr William Gorman KC prosecuting pointed to the incriminating statement made after his arrest, but mainly to the damning fingerprint evidence left at the scene of the crime. Gorman dismissed any claims of insanity by showing how Griffiths had covered his tracks by lying about his whereabouts and movements on the night of the murder.

Agreeing with the prosecution, the three-day trial ended when the jury took just twenty-three minutes to bring in a verdict of guilty. Griffiths stood unmoved as sentence of death was passed on him.

Had his trial been scheduled for a few weeks earlier, then Griffiths would not have hanged. Throughout the period of the murder investigation and for a month either side, all persons sentenced to death had automatically been reprieved while the latest debate on the death penalty was heard in Parliament.

Perhaps Griffiths preferred death to a life in prison. Whilst on remand at Walton gaol he had to make an appearance at a court hearing. The journey was made in the prison van, a notoriously bumpy ride that caused nausea in many prisoners and escorts. Arriving at the court he asked for a drink and was given a glass of water. As he put the glass to his lips, Detective Sergeant Ernie Millen saw a strange look come over the prisoner's face and quickly knocked the glass out of his hand onto the floor. Griffiths confessed that he had planned to smash the glass and cut his own throat.

The suspension of all death sentences had ended by the time Griffiths took his place in the condemned cell at Walton gaol, and on Friday morning, 19th November 1948, he was hanged by Albert Pierrepoint and Harry Allen. Pierrepoint noted that he met his end bravely – like a soldier.

Over 46,000 fingerprint cards where ceremoniously pulped on 3rd November in a Blackburn paper mill, in the presence of the town's mayor, hundreds of citizens, police and newspaper photographers. Five hundred or so of the fingerprint cards were not destroyed. Instead they were kept as ghoulish souvenirs of one of the biggest fingerprint hunts in criminal history.

LIFE FOR A LIFE

The murder of Amanda Graham at Southport, May 1961

There is a strange anomaly concerning the debate on the re-introduction of the death penalty. Even today, many people who claim to support its abolition would consider bringing it back for child killers. And yet, despite all the newspaper campaigns and media calls each time a child is brutally murdered, under the Homicide Act of 1957, child murder was one of the types of murder deemed no longer worthy of the death penalty. If it wasn't for this Act, the brutal killer of a young girl in a Southport hotel room in the summer of 1961 would now be lying in a felon's grave at Liverpool's Walton gaol, rather than being the second-longest detained prisoner currently held in captivity.

Amanda Graham was 6 years old. Mandy, as she preferred to be known, lived with her parents, older brother and sister on Hartford Road, Southport. It was Wednesday, 24th May, a warm summer evening in 1961, when Mandy, a friendly and talkative child, asked her mother if she could go to the amusement park, Pleasureland, with her friends Freda and Linda. As both the girls were considerably older than Mandy, Veronica Graham agreed and watched from her shellfish stall as Mandy, wearing her school blazer, skipped happily out of the market hall. As darkness fell and she failed to return home, her parents became concerned and phoned the police. A missing person's enquiry took a more sinister turn when the police learnt from several witnesses that Mandy had been seen on a number of occasions that evening in the company of a mysterious man. Various witnesses stated that they saw Mandy holding his hand as they

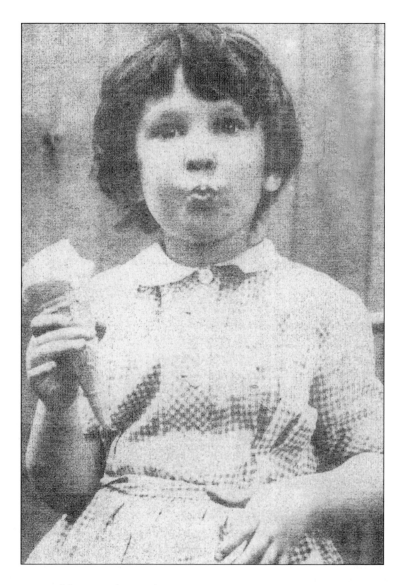

Six-year-old Amanda Graham.

walked down the promenade; another saw her perched on his shoulders as they strolled towards the Manchester road.

Police with tracker dogs hurried to the scene and officers from neighbouring forces gave assistance. Soon the police had a name for this mystery man: he was identified as Alan Victor Wills, a 33-year-old hotel and kitchen porter at the Palace Hotel, Birkdale. Officers raced to the hotel but found his room locked, and when told he was off duty they left to pursue enquiries elsewhere.

The search through the night proved fruitless and descriptions of Mandy and Wills were posted to staff at air and seaports, bus and railway stations. He was described as five foot three inches tall, with dark brown hair and a hooked nose. More noticeable was a withered right hand that left his arm noticeably shorter than the other, and he was heavily tattooed on his arms and hands. Mandy was described as having bobbed brown hair and wearing a Holy Trinity school uniform and blazer. Officers visited scores of hotels and boarding houses to see if anyone matching these descriptions had checked in, without success.

Wills was a native of Royton, near Oldham. Detectives contacted the Oldham Police to ask them to be on the lookout in case he had abducted Mandy and taken her there. He was also known to have friends in Chesterfield and a search was made there, too.

At 9.25 am the next morning Wills reported for duty at the kitchen but on hearing that the police had called on the previous evening looking for him, he made some excuse, returned to his room and then disappeared. Tipped off that Wills had been seen, Detective Sergeant Mackenzie Folan called at the hotel. He was led to room 13 in the staff quarters and knocked on the door. Receiving no answer he put his shoulder to the flimsy hotel door and forced it open. Under the bed, covered in a man's clothing, was the naked and sexually violated body of the young girl.

Heading what had now become a murder hunt, Chief Constable Joe Pessell assigned every available man on the case. Home Office Pathologist Dr Charles St Hill carried out a post mortem and confirmed that cause of death was asphyxia from pressure on the neck and that prior to death she had been raped.

The Palace Hotel in Birkdale (now demolished) where Alan Wills worked as a porter.

Wills was at liberty for less than twenty-four hours once the manhunt began, and was soon traced to a house at Mawdesley on the outskirts of Wigan. He made a statement in which he said that he remembered nothing after leaving the Fisherman's Rest. 'I am ashamed of everything . . . I just woke up and seen her laid out on the bed.'

Standing trial at Liverpool Assizes, before Mr Justice Atkinson in early November that year, there was never much doubt as to his actual guilt. Statements he had made upon arrest and at a subsequent hearing confirmed he was the killer: what the court needed to decide now was if he was suffering from diminished responsibility or guilty as charged.

Leading for the prosecution, Mr Alexander Karmel QC outlined the facts. He said that Amanda had left Pleasureland at around 7 pm and had boarded a bus with her two friends. Wills was also a passenger on the bus and when Amanda alighted from the bus in Leyton Road, at the stop before her friends would get off, Will followed her off the bus. A witness saw them talking and another saw them holding hands along the road. Amanda seemed happy and was smiling and they were engaged in conversation.

At a few minutes to 10 pm they were seen by a girl who knew them both, and asked why Mandy was not home at that time of night. Wills told her he was taking her home now and she watched them walk in the right direction for Mandy's home.

'Unfortunately, members of the jury,' Karmel said, 'Amanda was not taken home.'

Her parents reported her missing at 10.15 pm. He went on to describe the finding of the body by Detective Sergeant Folan. Folan told the court how he had found the youngster bound and partially naked, and the pathologist took the stand to say that during the course of a serious sexual assault she had been asphyxiated by pressure applied to her throat.

Defending the prisoner, Mr Leslie Rigg QC addressed the court and said that he was not in a position to contest the Crown's version of events as Wills was convinced that he must have carried out the 'brutal act', but that he had no idea of carrying it out. He then asked the jury to consider the state of Wills' mind at the time of the assault. Medical evidence was called to support Rigg's suggestion that Wills was suffering from some mental illness. Dr Sharpe from the local Birkdale hospital said he had examined Wills and that in normal conversation he was cheerful, co-operative and apparently normal. He did, however, possess a mental age of around eleven and was, in the doctor's opinion, borderline between definite sub normality and 'the low average'.

Further medical evidence was called from Dr Gray, the senior medical officer at Liverpool's Walton gaol. He told the court he felt that Wills was feigning illness: 'I formed the opinion that he knew more than he cared to admit or was willing to discuss about the events of 24th May.'

The medical evidence took up the bulk of the case and it was left for the judge to summarise the facts and explain the legal situation regarding the medical conditions as they had been suggested in court. In one of the most dramatic summing ups ever heard in a court of law, Mr Justice Atkinson asked the jury to consider if while carrying out the brutal sexual assault on his victim Wills had intentionally strangled her.

Holding his wristwatch in his hand he asked the jury to consider if fifteen seconds was a long time to choke the child. The silence hung heavy in the court until it was finally broken by his lordship. 'It is quite a long time. It is for you to decide if a man chokes a child for fifteen seconds he has an understanding of what he has done'. He told them that if they believed he did have an understanding then he was guilty of murder, if he didn't, then they could find a verdict of manslaughter through diminished responsibility.

After less than forty minutes on the second day of the trial, the jury of ten men and two women returned a verdict of guilty, and Wills was sentenced to life imprisonment. He will probably spend the rest of his life behind bars.

FOR ME AND MY GIRL

The murder of James Littler at Clitheroe, January 1964

The early 1960s were a time of change in attitudes towards crime and punishment. After a series of high profile, controversial executions in the mid-1950s, including those of Ruth Ellis and Derek Bentley, there was a feeling across the land that the death penalty had had its day. Following the Homicide Act of 1957 that categorised between capital and non-capital murder, it usually took an exceptionally vicious murder to send the killer to the gallows. In the years that followed the Homicide Act, there was on average less than five executions a year.

One murder that many people felt deserved the ultimate punishment was that of retired James Littler. Having been wounded in the First World War, Littler bore his wounds bravely and was able to spend most of his working life as a builder and bricklayer in Clitheroe. In the early 1950s he retired from the building trade and lived on his own as a watch-repairer in his cosy terraced house on Derby Street.

On the afternoon of Thursday, 30th January 1964, Littler had a visitor at the house. The caller shared a cup of tea then left, but not before battering the old man to death with a half-brick and a heavy brass candlestick.

A neighbour made the gruesome discovery when he called round to drop off a watch for repair. Receiving no answer to his persistent knocking, he tried the front door, found it open and upon entering the house was met with a scene of devastation. Littler

The house in Derby Street where James Littler lived and worked.

was lying on the floor in a pool of blood with his coat covering his head.

Soon police were cordoning off the house as a full-scale murder hunt swung into place. Pathologist Dr John Benstead carried out a post mortem and found that cause of death was from cerebral haemorrhaging, as a result of several violent blows to the head.

Detective Chief Superintendent Roberts immediately set out a plan to visit every one of the 5,000 homes in the area. In a move that echoed the detective work that helped solve the Blackburn Hospital murder of 1948, he announced that he would fingerprint every male over the age of sixteen.

Teams of detectives began door-to-door enquiries, each armed with the same six questions:

1. Did you know James Littler?
2. When did you last see him alive?
3. Have you ever visited his home, and if so how often and when was the last time?
4. Were you in the vicinity of Derby Street between 5 pm and midnight on Thursday, 30th January 1964?
5. Did you see anyone acting suspiciously?
6. Do you know anyone who was in the habit of visiting Mr Littler?

They soon had a result. As Roberts' team sifted through the first set of statements, one name cropped up several times as having been seen in the vicinity of Derby Street at the time of the murder: Joseph Wilson Masters, a 22-year-old coalman, whose round took in Derby Street. He would have had legitimate work reasons for being in the area at the time of the murder, and a check into his record found that he had convictions for violence.

His employer, however, said that Masters would not have been working on that street as he had left the company and was probably out of work. However, he did remember a remark Masters had made recently when, after finishing his shift and returning to the depot, he had mentioned that 'old man Littler seemed to have a lot of money and cigarettes...'

An old school friend of Masters told police that she had seen him in the Wheatsheaf Hotel on Thursday evening. Red-faced, as if had been running, he told her: 'They are after me! I have broken into my mother's gas meter, and I've had a fight with some bloke and got some money off him.' He then made some claims about it being lucky he was wearing gloves and said he had to go to the gents' toilets to try to wash the blood off his trousers. She told police that she didn't understand what he was talking about – and he often said things that she took with a pinch of salt! She did give the police one important lead though, telling them that Masters said he was planning to catch the 8.20 pm bus to Manchester.

Further investigations went on into the night and it was learnt that Masters had travelled to Manchester in the company of Patricia Pilkington, a 21-year-old cotton winder from Padiham. They were thought to be staying in the Ardwick area of Manchester. The Manchester police were issued with descriptions of the wanted couple. On Saturday night as they enjoyed a drink together, they were spotted by officers and Masters was arrested. Charging him with capital murder, Detective Inspector Thompson of the Manchester Police handed Masters the charge sheet. He skimmed through it and threw it down on the desk. 'Murder eh? Okay, I will tell you all about it.'

Masters made a statement to the effect that he and Patricia had been living together since 25th January. Three days later they went to Ardwick. On 30th January, with their finances running low, Masters had returned to Clitheroe to get some money. He returned later that night and said he had obtained some money, £6 or £7, and that he had had a fight which resulted in him getting bloodstains on his trousers.

On the following morning Patricia read a headline in the local paper about the Clitheroe murder, which he denied carrying out. He ended the statement by saying: 'I just wanted some money for me and my girl Pat so that we could go away and live like any other person would do'.

Joseph Masters stood trial for murder at Lancaster Assizes on 29th April, before Mr Justice Gorman. Godfrey Heilpern QC led for the prosecution, with Walter Hodgson QC for the defence. He was charged with capital murder (murder in the furtherance of theft) to which he pleaded not guilty. To the lesser charge of non-capital murder, a charge that carried only a custodial sentence as opposed to the gallows if convicted of the former, he chose to plead guilty.

Masters told how he had become friendly with James Littler to whom he delivered coal on his rounds. The two had become chatty and on more than one occasion the old man had lent him small sums of money which he had paid back in full on pay day. He said that on 30th January their funds had run low and during a discussion with Patricia Pilkington, she had asked him if he knew anyone in Clitheroe who could lend them money. He mentioned the old man and she accompanied him to the bus station while he went in search of the money. Aware that they would have no room for the night if he failed to return with any money, Masters had told her, as he left, to contact the police if he wasn't on the last bus back, as he didn't want her walking the streets.

Arriving at the house, Masters said that the old man let him in and made a pot of tea. He asked about Littler giving him a loan of a couple of pounds. Things however had changed since the last time. Masters no longer worked on the coal wagon and was therefore no longer a weekly visitor to the houses, and being out of work, even if it was only temporary, meant he didn't have the means to repay the debt.

'I told him I was going to make a fresh start,' Masters said, promising to repay the money at the first chance he could.

'He paused for a moment then a strange laugh came over his face. He then gave me a lecture that I should be working like everyone else. He then brought Pat into it. I told him that she was expecting and again he laughed.'

It was at this point that Masters lost his temper.

'He said I should be more careful, he began to swear, then said in a scornful voice "you will get nothing from me".' He then described how Littler continued to mock him and finally his patience snapped. He picked up a half-brick that happened to be beside the door and rained it down on his head several times, oblivious to the old man's cries.

'I don't remember much after that ... it was very blurred ... I remember looking down at him and it took me a few moments to realise what I had done.'

Masters said that he tried to revive the old man and turned out a number of drawers looking for bandages. But it was too late. 'I did not take anything out of the house and I had no intention of doing so,' he remarked to the hushed court. He then covered the man's face with his jacket and slipped out of the house.

Having failed in his quest to get the money by legitimate means, Masters tried an alternative scheme. He called at his mother's house and, as she was out, climbed in through the window. He washed the blood from his hands and cleaned up his clothes the best he could, before breaking open the gas meter and putting around £7 worth of coins into a sock.

Asked by the prosecution why, if he knew that he had left the old man dead on the floor, he had told his girlfriend this wasn't the case. He said he didn't want to upset her and he wasn't totally sure the man was dead when he left.

Now came the crux of the case. Mr Heilpern said that Masters was a ruthless, cold-bloodied killer who had gone to the house on Derby Street wearing gloves with the intention of obtaining money by force. 'Why else would he go there wearing gloves, if it wasn't to steal and to disguise his fingerprints?' he asked the jury.

The defence countered the claim that he had gone there to steal, by pointing out that before leaving the house he had placed the victim's jacket over his face and at no time did he search his pockets where he would have found some money. Likewise, a jacket hanging on a chair in the living room contained a wallet with over £10 in it and there was over £20 in a drawer in the bedroom.

The prosecution contested this issue, pointing to the ransacked state of the house. It suggested that any money left behind at the house was more by luck than design. Masters was panicking while he searched for money and in his haste had failed to spot several quantities of cash.

Summing up on the third day of the trial, Mr Justice Gorman outlined the key points in relation to the charges facing the prisoner in the dock. He told the jury they had three options. The first option was that they could bring in a verdict of manslaughter, if they considered he had suffered sufficient provocation. He countered this by saying that a man with a short and violent temper could not plead guilty to manslaughter simply because he had been provoked.

The second option was that if they believed Masters went to that house with the intention to steal, whether he stole or not, then that would be deemed capital murder. The final choice they had was if they believed he had killed Mr Littler for any other reason then it would be non-capital murder.

The jury took less than three hours to find him guilty on point number two: that he had committed murder in the course or furtherance of theft. Mr Justice Gorman sentenced Masters to death and added that he had totally agreed with the jury's verdict.

Masters was removed to the condemned cell at Walton gaol and letters were sent out to hangman Harry Allen and his assistant Harry Robinson, engaging their services for the execution which was initially scheduled for Wednesday, 20th May.

Patricia Pilkington was allowed to visit Masters at Liverpool and tearfully told him that she still loved him and wanted to marry him. 'I think we had better wait until I know the result of my appeal before we make any plans,' he wisely informed her from behind the toughened glass wall in the interview room.

An appeal was set for Thursday 14th May on the grounds that the judge had misdirected the jury on certain points in relation to the meaning of theft. The salient points of the trial were dissected again and, after deliberating for less than an hour, the panel concurred with the original verdict and returned Masters to the death cell. A new date of 5th June was set for the execution.

A petition for a reprieve in Masters' home town met with little support and on 1st June a request by members of the family to see the Home Secretary was also rejected. It seemed that Masters' fate was all but sealed. It had been a terrible crime and the brutality in which it had been carried out was far worse than others in recent times in which the killers had gone to the gallows. Masters and his family were warned to expect the worst.

It was to be some surprise then when, on the stroke of midnight just seventy-two hours before he was scheduled to die, the Governor entered the condemned cell at Walton and informed Masters that he had been reprieved. On the following afternoon he was visited again by Patricia Pilkington to whom he proposed marriage. 'It's the happiest day of my life,' she said to reporters outside the gaol.

Joseph Wilson Masters was the last man sentenced to death in Lancashire. Many people thought that the willingness to reprieve such a brutal killer as Masters heralded the death knell for capital punishment, and it is recorded by one senior policeman as his belief that no one would be hanged in Great Britain again. The contrariness of the whole system of handing out reprieves to condemned murderers is only too clearly illustrated here. Less than a month after Masters was reprieved, two death sentences were passed at Manchester Assizes on a pair of Preston dairymen, Peter Allen and Gwynne Evans who had committed murder in the course of theft at a house in Workington. The cases were in many ways similar, and there seemed no reason to differentiate between this case and the Masters one. Allen and Evans went into the record books as the last two to hang; Joseph Masters, who killed because he wanted money 'for me and my girl' went on to serve fifteen and a half years, receiving his freedom in November 1979.

THE MOST HAUNTED HOUSE?

The mysterious sightings at Chingle Hall, Goosnargh, near Preston

Chingle Hall, amongst the oldest inhabited brick buildings in Great Britain, stands at Goosnargh, an old Viking village not far from Preston. Built around 1260 by a knight called Adam de Singleton, it was originally named Singleton Hall. Singleton was a devout Catholic and had a chapel built at the house. The Singleton family lived there for over 300 years and it is Eleanor Singleton who is said to be one of the most active of the alleged 16 spirits who haunt the house, and it is her room that is considered to be the most haunted. It was in this room that 8-year-old Eleanor Singleton was reportedly held captive for over 12 years. She died (some suggest she was murdered) at the age of 20 and guests have claimed to be overcome by a deep feeling of sadness when in this room. On occasions a figure has been experienced tugging at the bedclothes, mystical orbs have materialised and a strong smell of lavender has been reported. Some guests staying in the room have been so overcome with terror that they have fainted.

In 1585, the Wall family, relatives of the Singletons, moved into the Hall, and a member of this family is thought to be a most prominent spirit there. John Wall was born here in 1620, in what had by now become known as Chingle Hall. He later studied at Worcester University and at the age of 21 became a priest. These were

Chingle Hall is no longer open to the public.

dangerous times: during the Catholic Reformation it was illegal to celebrate mass in England, but for many years Chingle Hall was used as a place of worship. Concealed around the Hall were a number of secret compartments or priest holes, where those taking part in the mass rushed to hide if the Hall was raided by Royalist soldiers. In the early days of the civil war, Father John Wall was one of the most active priests, regularly conducting secret masses.

In 1678, albeit with the monarchy restored, Wall was arrested at Rushock Court near Bromsgrove, as he was tendering the Oath of Supremacy. Taken to Worcester gaol, Wall was told that his life would be spared if he would denounce his religion. He declined and was sentenced to be drawn and quartered, the last man in Worcestershire to be condemned for his faith. Following his execution at Redhill on 22nd August 1679, his dismembered body was handed over to his friends who interred it in a nearby churchyard. The severed head was retained by friars at Worcester, who later took it around the country on a reverential tour before returning it to Chingle Hall the following year. It is thought that the head was either buried in the grounds or secreted somewhere in the house.

John Wall was later canonised, and is said to appear within the house and gardens. There have been numerous recorded sightings of a strange, hooded monk walking slowly and forlornly. Although it is commonly thought that the severed head has been secreted at Chingle Hall, another story says that it was taken to France, and that if his head were returned to Chingle Hall the haunting would cease. There is also the legend that Father John Wall left his own story:

> *This was my birthplace and I return here to find comfort. I do not regret my beliefs. I am proud that I was one of the last Roman Catholic Martyrs. I hope I didn't die in vain. After they executed me, my head was struck from my body and sent to France. Some kind souls brought it back and buried it in the grounds of my beloved Chingle Hall, so that I may rest in peace.*

In 1764, the house passed to the Farrington family and Chingle Hall continued as a hive of zealous religious activity. Great efforts were made to keep celebrating the Roman Catholic mass, cavities were built into walls and tunnels were dug to some of the surrounding buildings as a method of escape if needed.

Over the next two centuries the Hall passed through a succession of owners, all of whom reported sinister apparitions and occurrences. During the 1950s, one of the large wooden roof beams, purportedly taken from Viking longboats, spontaneously caught fire, and, just as quickly, inexplicably extinguished itself: the smell of burning wood still lingers in many of the rooms. There is also supposedly a poltergeist in the kitchen that will startle nervous cooks by rearranging the pots and pans.

Upstairs is what is known as the priests' room and, from its window, a man with shoulder length hair has been seen many times walking outside the window. This might not seem too unusual, if it wasn't for the fact that the window is over 13 feet above ground.

If the strange sightings, unexplained fires and poltergeist activities weren't enough, there has also been unusual sounds reported in the house. One Christmas Day over 25 years ago, two ghost-hunters spent time at the Hall, and recorded knocking sounds emanating from one of the former priest's hideaways. Besides the knocking noises they recorded a considerable drop in temperature and saw an 'indefinable shape' move across the floor.

In January 1996, members of the Northern Anomalies Research Organisation investigated Chingle Hall and, during a visit, one member of the group managed to capture on photograph a blue/white light on and near the oak-beamed ceiling. This photographic evidence was corroborated by a number of witnesses at the Hall, and, when tape recorders were used in an investigation, unexplained sounds were recorded within the priest's room.

Other noises have been heard throughout the house: tapping sounds on the walls, doors creaking open of their own accord and, most common of all, the sound of footsteps. Numerous guests throughout the years have reported hearing footsteps in corridors when there was no one around, and on one occasion in modern times, nine people, including the then owners, heard footsteps tramping through what has been named the 'haunted room'. It is in this room that a hooded monk has also been seen.

In the summer of 1968, two young boys sleeping in the 'haunted room', claimed to have heard footsteps and knockings during the night. They also saw a strange light appear in the centre of the room; it moved around for a while before it disappeared into the wall.

Other visitors have recorded the sounds of bricks being moved in the priest's room, which again seem to originate in the hiding hole. One guest, peering into the hole, claimed to see part of a human hand moving one of the bricks and, as he watched, the movement stopped and the hand disappeared. This same witness was also able to capture the sounds of footsteps on tape and record the faint image of a hooded monk on film. On the same occasion bricks were later found strewn across the floor of the ground floor chapel.

For a time in the recent past, people interested in paranormal activity were able to book to stay the night at Chingle Hall. There were so many recordings of sightings that it became unusual to visit the house and not see a ghost!

One visitor reported that his 14-year-old niece and a friend were assailed by a number of malicious spirits. The events were so bad that a resident tour guide was ready to quit her job. Ruefully summing up his visit to the Hall he said: 'The only way I can describe it is we went to see a bonfire and got well and truly burned!'

Chingle Hall is no longer opened to the public.

THE KILLER OF
JACK THE RIPPER?

---------------❀---------------

The murder of James Maybrick at Aigburth, 1889

Florence Elizabeth Chandler had first met James Maybrick on board the White Star liner *SS Baltic* on 12th March, 1880. She had left her home in Mobile, Alabama, for a trip to Paris with her thrice-married mother, Baroness Caroline Chandler von Roques and her older brother, Holbrook. On the second day of the Atlantic crossing, Holbrook got into conversation with James Maybrick and, finding they shared mutual business interests, they spent many hours in the first class tearoom. Holbrook introduced his new friend to his young sister and there was an instant attraction between the pair.

James Maybrick was a successful, Liverpool cotton merchant who spent much of each year in Norfolk, Virginia. At 42 years old he was a wealthy and popular businessman. Florie, as she preferred to be known, was impulsive, headstrong and at the age of just 17 over 20 years younger than the polite and mild-mannered Maybrick. Oblivious to gossip, they spent the majority of the eight-day voyage in each other's company and by the time the ship reached Liverpool Florie, perhaps influenced by her scheming mother, had decided that she wanted to marry the wealthy cotton merchant.

Maybrick altered his plans and soon followed Florie to Paris where they continued a relationship that led to marriage in the summer of 1881. They chose to live in America for the first three years, before returning to England in 1884.

The impulsive and headstrong Florence Chandler. *James Maybrick, a successful cotton merchant.*

By 1887, they had settled into the grandly-named Battlecrease House at Aigburth, a suburb on the outskirts of Liverpool overlooking the River Mersey. By now they had two children: James 'Bobo' Chandler born in 1882, and Gladys Evelyn, born in 1885. Although their marriage appeared on the surface to be a happy one, cracks had begun to appear. Florie soon found out that her husband had kept a number of secrets from her. As a result of his frequent travelling to America before his marriage, he had contracted malaria. His treatment had consisted of an arsenic-based preparation, and when Maybrick recovered from the disease, he found he was addicted to the medicine. He became reliant on the white, powdery ingredients of Fowler's Medicine (a concoction of arsenic and strychnine), adding it to tonics and slipping it into his food. He confessed his addiction to her when she uncovered a number of packages of white powder hidden amongst his clothes.

After exposing one of his secrets, she soon discovered what many of their friends already knew: her husband had a mistress who lived in the Whitechapel district of London. Maybrick had been seeing this woman long before he married and she had borne him a number of children, many of whom died in infancy.

Adding to their woes, the cotton business was in trouble and moving to the grand house had caused them to live above their means. Tensions soon developed between husband and wife. These came to a head when Florie discovered that her husband was sending maintenance payments of over £100 a year to his mistress.

Florie was furious and banned James from her bed. As their marriage deteriorated, Maybrick became a fully-fledged arsenic

Battlecrease House.

addict, visiting his local chemist as many as five times a day to purchase his 'pick-me-up tonics'. The tonics were now beginning to affect Maybrick's personality. He became aggressive, short-tempered and on more than one occasion he beat his wife.

Despondent of her home situation, Florie began an affair with a family friend, Alfred Brierly. Victorian England was one of double standards. Despite Maybrick having been embroiled in an extra-marital relationship for over a decade, upon discovering that his wife had a lover and that many of their friends already knew about it, he was mortified. He attacked Florie and gave her a black eye.

By June 1888, Maybrick began to experience health problems. Aware that Maybrick was something of a hypochondriac, Dr Hopper, the family doctor, thought nothing untoward of his sudden ill health. All told, Maybrick made close on 20 visits to the surgery between June and September. The doctor knew that Maybrick was suffering from years of drug abuse, but seemed content to placate his patient and merely prescribed more doses of arsenic and strychnine.

Aware that his medication was beginning to ruin his life, Maybrick decided to cease taking such huge doses and cut back on his intake of arsenic during the spring of 1889. It was known even then that to suddenly stop after such a long-term addiction could be fatal.

In April 1889, having misplaced her prescription for an arsenic-based cosmetic face wash, Florie made up a concoction herself by soaking flypaper to distil the arsenic. She made no effort to disguise what she was doing. By early May, when James's condition began to deteriorate, Nurse Alice Yapp, one of the domestic staff, confided in a family friend who summoned Maybrick's brother Michael, a famous composer living in London. Michael Maybrick took charge. Seeing his brother was seriously ill, and knowing of the scandal of Florie and her lover, he immediately arranged for his brother's will to be changed so that Florie would not benefit from it. He was also given the authority to handle his brother's estate.

Still Florie continued her affair. She wrote to Alfred Brierly and asked Alice Yapp to mail the letter. Walking to the post office with the nurse, her daughter Gladys dropped it into a puddle. Picking up the soaking letter Alice Yapp, who was already suspicious of her mistress's relationship with Brierly, opened it and read the contents.

'*Dearest* ...

I cannot answer your letter fully today, my darling, but relieve your mind of all ... fear of discovery now and in the future. M. has been delirious since Sunday, and I know now that he is perfectly ignorant of everything ... Excuse this scrawl, my own darling, but I dare not leave the room for a moment, and I do not know when I shall be able to write to you again.

In haste, yours ever. Florie

Brierly never received the letter; Alice Yapp instead handed it to Michael Maybrick.

As James's condition worsened and he was unable to digest food easily, his doctors prescribed meat juice. During the evening of 9th May, he asked Florie to add some of 'my powder' to the juice. Two days later, James Maybrick died and within hours Florie became a prisoner in her own home. Michael Maybrick had taken charge. The police were summoned and three days later, after making a series of enquiries, Florence was arrested for the murder of her husband.

An inquest was held on 13th May, and found death was due to 'inflammation of the stomach and bowels set up by some irritant poison'.

When the case came to the assizes, at Liverpool on 1st August 1889, fate seemed to conspire against Florence Maybrick. Her mother had hired barrister Sir Charles Russell, a brilliant lawyer in his prime, but by 1889 his glory days were well behind him and his recent record showed a string of high profile defeats. Worse still was the choice of judge. Mr Justice Stephen, although once highly respected, by now one or two questions were being asked about his mental state.

The trial was to last seven days. The Crown put forward its case that the accused had murdered her husband for financial gain and to be free to carry on her adulterous relationship. Her defence failed to inform the court as to the extent of Maybrick's addiction to arsenic and strychnine. The prosecution had alluded to the fact Maybrick was addicted to arsenic but not to what extent.

Although the defence had already made one serious blunder over its failure to exploit the point that Maybrick might have been

Sir Charles Russell was hired as the defence lawyer.

responsible for his own demise through an overdose, they made a further and fatal error when they allowed Florence Maybrick to make a statement to the court. If it was an attempt to help persuade them of her innocence it backfired spectacularly. She admitted her adultery to the court and in so doing condemned herself the moment she opened her mouth.

During summing up, judges are allowed to comment on the evidence, usually with delicate care, but Mr Justice Stephen bluntly acknowledged that he abhorred Florie's adultery. The summary took two of the seven days, and was clearly biased against the accused. Following the judge's comments, it took the jury just 35 minutes to find Florence Maybrick guilty of murder.

There was no Court of Criminal Appeals in 1889 and realistically only Queen Victoria could save Florence Maybrick. She was not known as a compassionate monarch, and it was not until a huge public groundswell of support, following numerous petitions for clemency, did she act. On 23rd August, four days before she was scheduled to hang, the Home Secretary issued an order that spared her life, sentencing her instead to life in prison.

From the moment of her arrest Florence Maybrick never saw her children again, Michael Maybrick saw to that. Even when the children were old enough to make decisions for themselves, despite their mother's efforts, they refused any contact with her.

The Maybrick case had a dramatic impact on the criminal justice system and it was instrumental in the setting up of a court of appeal. It was not however until 1907, that this was established.

Florence Chandler was set free on 4th January 1904 after serving almost 15 years. She spent six months in a convent in Truro, Cornwall before sailing back with her mother to America. Under the name Florence Elizabeth Chandler, she later wrote a book about her ordeal: *My Lost Fifteen Years*. She died, aged 79, in Connecticut on 23rd October 1941.

But that is not quite the end of the story.

In 1993, a dramatic discovery stunned the world when a diary was unearthed suggesting that James Maybrick was 'Jack the Ripper', the infamous murderer of Whitechapel. The diary, allegedly the work of

James Maybrick, had been found during a house refurbishment and it gave graphic descriptions of the murders committed by the Ripper, including, some historians claimed, details that could only have been known by the actual murderer.

A pocket watch, purchased by a Liverpool grandfather, and similar to one Maybrick was known to have worn, was also discovered in a Liverpool antique shop. The watch had superficial scratches on the inside cover which when viewed under a microscope revealed the signature: 'J. Maybrick'.

Also allegedly on the case were the words *I am Jack* scratched across the centre of the cover. Etched around the edge were the initials of the victims of Jack the Ripper.

Linking Maybrick to Whitechapel, the scene of the Ripper's murders, was easy. His mistress had lived there for many years and as he was a frequent visitor, he knew the area well. This was something the police were convinced of, as the killer was able to slip away into the labyrinth of side streets and passages that a stranger to the area would probably not be aware of. Also, an 1888 police drawing of the Ripper, based on eyewitness reports, looked similar to photographs of a hatless James Maybrick.

That the diary was authentic and not a hoax, was treated with a certain amount of scepticism; with many of the world's leading 'Ripperologists' openly declaring that the diary was a fraud.

The beginning of the diary is undated and seems to start mid-thought: ... *They will suffer just as I ... until I have sought my revenge on the whore and the whoremaster.* The writer refers to his brothers (who share the same names as Maybrick's brothers) and his children (Gladys and Bobo). 'The whore' is alleged to be Florie Maybrick and the 'whore master' her lover, Brierley.

He called his string of killings 'my campaign' and claimed that before terrorising Whitechapel, he tested 'his stomach for murder' in Manchester. No murder in Manchester was ever associated with Jack the Ripper, but as it took place, if indeed it did, before the wave of Ripper killings, there is no reason why it should have been.

The contemporary papers and all the Ripper stories focus on the horrific crimes in Whitechapel. James Maybrick, assuming he was the Ripper, began his London terror on 31st August 1888. His first victim was 42-year-old Mary Ann ('Polly') Nichols. Maybrick claimed he continued to take his arsenic and strychnine in ever-increasing amounts to gain strength for his 'campaign.'

Just over a week later, Annie Chapman became his next victim. At 47, she was already suffering from a terminal disease before she met her grisly end. The Ripper earned his self-described nickname on the night he killed Annie Chapman. Within three weeks he struck again. Elizabeth Stride was found dead in the early hours of 30th September, but before the Ripper could live up to his name, a passer-by interrupted his work. In his diary, Maybrick wrote:

To my astonishment I cannot believe I have not been caught ...

The Ripper was saved, in his own estimation, by the panic of the witness.

... As I write I find it impossible to believe he did not see me ... the fool panicked, it is what saved me.

The diary goes on to say he had not been satisfied with that evening's work and less than an hour after the murder he struck again. Around the time the Ripper was murdering his third victim, Kate Eddowes was released from gaol, following an arrest for being drunk and disorderly. A witness saw her talking with a man whose description matched that of James Maybrick.

On the evening of 9th November, Mary Jane Kelly was found dead in a manner that shocked even the most hardened detectives. Gruesome pictures of the murder scene were widely published in the London papers. The horrific trail of murder ended as quickly as it had begun. According to his diary, he began to fear capture. *I cannot live without my medicine ... I see thousands of people chasing me, with Inspector Abberline in front dangling a rope.*

Thinking that London had become unsafe for him, Maybrick wrote that he had decided to commit another murder in Manchester.

I am tired and fear the city of whores has become too dangerous for I to return ... My first was in Manchester so why not my next?

According to Maybrick's diary, he found a Manchester victim the week after Christmas, 1888. *I could not cut like my last, visions of*

her flooded back to me as I struck ... I left her for dead that I know ... It did not amuse me. There was no thrill ...
The thrill of killing had finally left him.

As Maybrick's condition continued to worsen through the spring of 1889, he wrote the last entry in his diary. It is dated 3rd May 1889:

Soon, I trust, I shall be laid beside my dear mother and father I place this [the diary] now in a place were it shall be found. I pray whoever should read this will find it in their heart to forgive me ... yours truly Jack the Ripper Dated this third day of May 1889.

When James Maybrick died, did he take the secrets of the Whitechapel murders to his grave? Was he murdered by his wife, or did he finally overdose on the 'pick-me-ups' he had been addicted to for many years, the dosage of which he had increased at a worrying rate?

Is the diary authentic? Many experts disagree. They point to the handwriting being dissimilar to that known to belong to Maybrick. However, chemical tests on the ink and paper prove that if it is a forgery it is a very elaborate one and dates back to around the turn of the century.

The evidence against Maybrick is compelling, but the jury is still out on this important question. Was Florence Maybrick the killer of Jack the Ripper?